CP STUDY GUIDE AND MOCK EXAMINATION

5th Edition

CP STUDY GUIDE AND MOCK EXAMINATION

5th Edition

Prepared by:
NALA—The Association of Paralegals • Legal Assistants
1516 S. Boston, Suite 200, Tulsa, Oklahoma 74119

Based on Study Aids and Examinations Donated by:
Virginia Koerselman-Newman, J. D., Attorney at Law
Hemmingway, South Carolina

Connie Kretchmer, Advanced Certified Paralegal
Omaha, Nebraska

The Association of
Legal Assistants • Paralegals

These sample questions represent the general nature of the Certified Paralegal examination. No representation is made as to whether or not these questions will actually appear on the examination. No representation is made as to whether study of this manual will ensure successful completion of the Certified Paralegal examination. These questions and answers are current at the time of publication.

In statutes, bar association-adopted guidelines, and Supreme Court rules among the states, the terms *paralegal* and *legal assistant* are used interchangeably. NALA also continues to use the terms interchangeably, recognizing, however, that in many geographic areas, there is a preference. In this publication, *paralegal* is used throughout.

CENGAGE
Learning®

Australia • Brazil • Japan • Korea • Mexico • Singapore • Spain • United Kingdom • United States

CP Study Guide and Mock Examination, Fifth Edition
NALA—The Association of Paralegals/ Legal Assistants

Vice President and General Manager-Skills and Planning: Dawn Gerrain

Senior Product Manager: Shelley Esposito

Senior Director, Development-Skills and Planning: Marah Bellegarde

Senior Product Development Manager: Larry Main

Senior Content Developer: Melissa Riveglia

Product Assistant: Diane E. Chrysler

Director, Market Development Manager: Deborah Yarnell

Brand Manager: Kay Stefanski

Senior Market Development Manager: Erin Brennan

Senior Production Director: Wendy Troeger

Production Manager: Mark Bernard

Content Project Management and Art Direction: PreMediaGlobal

Senior Technology Project Manager: Joe Pliss

Media Editor: Deborah Bordeaux

Cover Image: ©Kompaniets Taras/shutterstock

For product information and technology assistance, contact us at **Professional & Career Group Customer Support, 1-800-648-7450**

For permission to use material from this text or product, submit all requests online at **cengage.com/permissions** Further permissions questions can be e-mailed to **permissionrequest@cengage.com**

Library of Congress Control Number: 2013936221

ISBN-13: 978-1-285-19324-3

Cengage Learning
200 First Stamford Place, 4th Floor
Stamford, CT 06902
USA

Cengage Learning products are represented in Canada by Nelson Education, Ltd.

To learn more about Cengage Learning, visit **www.cengage.com**

Visit our corporate website at **cengage.com**

Printed in the United States of America
1 2 3 4 5 6 7 17 16 15 14 13

CONTENTS

PART 3
Certified Paralegal Program
Mock Examination

INTRODUCTION

Shortly after its incorporation in 1975, NALA (the National Association of Legal Assistants, Inc.) addressed a primary reason for its formation—the establishment of national professional standards for the paralegal career field. The development of professional standards serves to define and provide direction in the dynamic growth and acceptance of the paralegal career field. After examining the work of professional associations and the purposes and successes of voluntary certification programs, NALA members determined that a certification examination process is the best and most meaningful way to address this goal.

The Certified Paralegal program is the result of this initial work. This program has enabled the profession to develop a strong and responsive self-regulatory program offering a nationwide credential paralegals. The Certified Paralegal program establishes and serves as:

- A standard of achievement and excellence for paralegals.
- A means of identifying those who have reached this standard of excellence.
- A national standard for paralegals, rather than fifty different standards for fifty different states.
- A program responsive to the needs of paralegals and responsive to the fact that self-regulation is needed to strengthen and expand development of this career field.
- A positive, ongoing, voluntary program to encourage the growth of the paralegal profession, attesting to and encouraging a high level of achievement, rather than serving as a barrier to entry into a profession.

Since administration of the first examination in 1976, the Certified Paralegal program has had a significant impact on the paralegal profession. For many paralegals, achievement of professional certification is a career goal. For others, immediately following completion of a paralegal training program, it is the final step in preparing for their career. And for others, it is a stepping stone to advanced certification in specific practice areas. For everyone in the field, it is a means of recognition and demonstration of competency.

The continued growth, development, and recognition of paralegals are critical elements to our profession. Each paralegal is enhanced by voluntary certification programs. Enhancement of the paralegal career field is the driving force of NALA.

PART
1

Certified Paralegal Exam
Mock Examination

General Description
Administrative Rules and Procedures

CERTIFIED PARALEGAL STUDY GUIDE AND MOCK EXAMINATION

To support legal assistants in pursuit of their certification, NALA offers study programs and materials designed to assist in individual study and preparation. This *Study Guide and Mock Examination* for the Certified Paralegal Examination is part of the educational offerings of the association.

This publication is divided into three parts. The first part is a brief description of the Certified Paralegal Examination.

The second part provides an outline for a 9-week group study program with weekly examinations. These examinations will serve as a starting point for further discussion and study.

The third part of this publication consists of a Certified Paralegal Mock Examination. Suggested testing times are indicated for each section. These sample questions represent the general nature of the Certified Paralegal Examination. No representation is made as to whether or not these questions will actually appear on the examination. While every effort is made to ensure that the answers given in the answer key are correct at the time of publication, verifying the answers through independent study is an excellent means of review and study.

STUDY REFERENCES

A list of suggested study references for the Certified Paralegal Examination appears in the outline of the weekly study sessions. This *Study Guide and Mock Examination* is an excellent companion to:

Certified Paralegal Review Manual: A Practical Guide to CP Exam Preparation, 4th Ed., by Koerselman-Newman, Virginia, J. D., in cooperation with the National Association of Legal Assistants, Inc.; Copyright 2014, Delmar, Cengage Learning.

Certified Paralegal preparation classes are also offered continuously by NALA. Visit the NALA Web site (www.nala.org)/Continuing Education/Online Education. These online review programs for the Certified Paralegal Examination include both live and self-study Web-based programs.

THE CERTIFIED PARALEGAL EXAMINATION

ADMINISTRATION

The Certifying Board for Paralegals was established by NALA in 1975 to administer a nationwide certification program. This Board is responsible for content, standards, and administration of the Certified Paralegal (CP) national program. It is composed of paralegals who have received the Certified Paralegal designation, attorneys, and paralegal educators. In the technical areas of statistical analyses, examination construction, reliability, and validity tests, the Board contracts with a professional consulting firm offering expertise in these areas as well as in occupational research. Technical analyses of the Certified Paralegal Examination are conducted on an ongoing basis to ensure the integrity of the examination. Content analyses of the test design, accuracy of questions, and topic/subject mix for each exam section are ongoing processes of the Certifying Board. The Board also utilizes the occupational data available through surveys of paralegals and other means, including review of textbooks and research within the field of paralegal education. Thus, the Board is assured that the examination reflects and responds to workplace realities and demands.

CERTIFICATION PROCESS

The Certified Paralegal Examination is a comprehensive examination administered at locations across the United States. The major subject areas of the examination are the following:

- Communications
- Ethics
- Judgment and Analytical Ability
- Legal Research
- Substantive Law, consisting of questions on:

    ___ American Legal System
    ___ Civil Litigation
    ___ Contracts
    ___ Business Organizations

The examination is updated continually. Knowledge and understanding of each of these areas is vital to the professional success and achievement of all paralegals regardless of individual specialty practice areas.

An essential element of the success of a paralegal is a general working knowledge of legal phrases and terms and common Latin phrases, as well as the correct understanding and utilization of these terms in written documents. Legal terminology has been incorporated into all sections of the Certified Paralegal Examination to test this knowledge, understanding, and utilization. Examinees are asked to demonstrate the different meanings of terms and identify terms through definitions or descriptions. Knowledge of general terms and phrases of major practice areas is tested under the substantive law sections.

The following references are the authorities for all definitions: *Black's Law Dictionary*, 9th Ed. (or most current) and *Merriam-Webster's Collegiate Dictionary*, 11th Ed. (or most current) G. & C. Merriam Company, Springfield, Massachusetts.

CONTINUING EDUCATION AND RECERTIFICATION

The Certified Paralegal designation is awarded for a period of 5 years. To maintain certified status, paralegals must submit proof of participation in a minimum of 50 hours of continuing legal education programs or individual study programs. Five of the 50 hours must be on the subject of legal ethics. No more than 10 hours of the 50 hours may be recorded for participation in seminar or classes in nonsubstantive law subject (such as law office management, computer program instruction, office technology). Credit is awarded for significant achievement in the area of continuing legal education, such as successful completion of a statewide certification test, completion of an Advanced Paralegal Certification Examination, or teaching. Specific requirements for recertification are furnished to certified paralegals upon successful completion of the certification examination. The CLE requirements are also available from NALA Headquarters and posted on the NALA Web site.

REVOCATION

The Certified Paralegal designation may be revoked for any of the following reasons:

1. Falsifying information on the application form
2. Being subsequently convicted of the unauthorized practice of law
3. Failing to meet continuing legal education requirements established by the Certifying Board
4. Divulging the contents of any examination question(s)
5. Being subsequently convicted of a felony
6. Violating the NALA Code of Ethics and Professional Responsibility
7. Violating the "Terms and Conditions of Testing"

GRADING

Once admitted to the Certified Paralegal credentialing program, examinees must successfully complete a five-part examination.

Effective with exams administered after January 1, 2013, the points required to pass each exam section is 73 percent of the total points available. The passing points, or cut scores, for the exams are established using a criterion-referenced technique. Qualified and trained Subject-Matter Experts (SMEs) participate in determining the passing points working with the psychometric consultant.

The final passing points resulting from this process are approved by the Certifying Board (or SME working group). The points required to pass each section may vary with each testing window.

Each exam section has proven to be well-defined content areas and clearly related to the work of paralegals. See the *Job Analysis Report* released in May 2012 on the NALA Web site under "Certification" and "About Paralegals."

The Certifying Board reserves the right to modify the maximum points allocated at any time, and will modify this report as changes occur.

Results of the examination are provided via U.S. mail to all examinees. The results will be released during the second week of the second month following the test window, that is, the second week of March, July, and November. This allows time for essays to be graded, data validated, and scores recorded. Results are not available by e-mail, telephone, or fax.

Grade reports provide failing scores only. In addition, examinees will receive a report of the subject areas that appear to be most difficult to them. This information is provided to assist examinees in preparation for their retake.

Grade reports do not provide passing scores. Sections of the examination that are successfully completed are designated with "Pass." The Certifying Board has determined that "Pass" is sufficient to designate successful completion of the examinations section and that if a paralegal has met the standard, the paralegal has earned the Certified Paralegal credential.

RETAKE POLICY

Applications for the Certified Paralegal Examination are considered active for a period of 2 years. During that time, all five sections of the examination must be successfully completed to achieve the Certified Paralegal credential. If the examination is not successfully completed within the 2-year period, credit for all completed sections will be forfeited and the entire examination must be retaken. A new, updated application form will be required. The 2-year period begins on the date any section of the examination is first taken.

Examinees who do not achieve a passing score on any sections(s) may retake the section(s) during any testing window within the 2-year period. Retake applications are due on the dates listed above for all applications.

ELIGIBILITY REQUIREMENTS

The term *legal assistant* is defined by NALA as follows:

> *Legal assistants are a distinguishable group of persons who assist attorneys in the delivery of legal services. Through formal education, training, and experience legal assistants have knowledge and expertise regarding the legal system and substantive and procedural law which qualify them to do work of a legal nature under the supervision of an attorney. (Within this occupational category, individuals are also known as "paralegals.")*
> Adopted by the NALA membership, July 1984.

In July 2001, the NALA membership voted to adopt the definition of the American Bar Association. It is as follows:

> *A legal assistant or paralegal is a person qualified by education, training or work experience who is employed or retained by a lawyer, law office, corporation, governmental agency or other entity who performs specifically delegated substantive legal work, for which a lawyer is responsible.*

In statutes, bar association–adopted guidelines, and supreme court rules among the states, the terms *paralegal* and *legal assistant* are used interchangeably. NALA also continues to use the terms interchangeably, recognizing, however, that in many geographic areas, there is a preference.

To be eligible for the Certified Paralegal Examination, a paralegal must meet one of the following alternate requirements:

1. Graduation from a paralegal program that is:
   a. Approved by the American Bar Association
   b. An associate degree program
   c. A postbaccalaureate certificate program in paralegal studies
   d. A bachelor's degree program in paralegal studies
   e. A paralegal program that consists of a minimum of 60 semester hours (or equivalent quarter or clock hours*) of which at least 15 semester hours (or equivalent quarter or clock hours**) are substantive legal courses.

   *900 clock hours is equivalent to 60 semester hours; 90 quarter hours is equivalent to 60 semester hours.
   **225 clock hours is equivalent to 15 semester hours; 22½ quarter hours is equivalent to 15 semester hours.

2. A bachelor's degree in any field plus 1 year's experience as a paralegal. Successful completion of at least 15 semester hours (or 22½ quarter hours or 225 clock hours) of substantive legal courses will be considered equivalent to 1 year's experience as a legal assistant/paralegal.
3. A high school diploma or equivalent plus 7 years' experience as a paralegal under the supervision of a member of the Bar, plus evidence of a minimum of 20 hours of continuing legal education credit to have been completed within a 2-year period prior to the examination date.

Individuals currently incarcerated for any offense or on probation, on parole, or under other court-imposed supervision for a felony offense are ineligible to sit for the Certified Paralegal Examination. Application forms and information concerning testing sites for the Certified Paralegal Examination are available from:

National Association of Legal Assistants, Inc.
1516 S. Boston Avenue, Suite #200
Tulsa, OK 74119
(918) 587-6828; fax (918) 582-6772
www.nala.org/certification.aspx

Detailed information and Certifying Board policies are posted on the NALA Web site at WWW.NALA.ORG.

TESTING CENTERS
The Certified Paralegal Examination is administered via a computer-based testing procedure.

PSI Testing Center Network
Most examinees in the CP program will be utilizing the PSI Premier PLUS and PSI Authorized Test Centers. Combined, there are over 500 PSI testing centers throughout the United States. After examinees are admitted to the CP program, they will work directly with PSI to confirm testing appointments. The Web site www. psiexams.com has a list of testing centers. Be sure to choose NALA as the sponsor name from the drop-down menu of certification programs for an accurate list.

Examinees Participating in Non-PSI Testing Centers
NALA has established procedures that allow an employer or school to apply to become a NALA-approved testing center. This is designed for groups of employees or paralegal students. A packet of forms and requirements to become an authorized testing center for the Certified Paralegal Examination is available from the NALA Web site and may also be obtained by contacting NALA Headquarters.

ADVANCED PARALEGAL CERTIFICATION

Once a paralegal has achieved the national Certified Paralegal credential, advanced certification is available to those seeking to further their education and training and to achieve recognition of this effort. While the Certified Paralegal credential is vital to many beginning their careers, advanced certification is important in career development and in addressing the changes that happen in professional life.

Work began in 2002 on a restructured advanced certification program that was introduced to the paralegal profession in July 2006. The new program is curriculum-based certification and is offered exclusively online. A certified paralegal is able to participate in a Web-based training program offering national certification in a variety of specialty areas of practice. An advanced certification credential is awarded to the paralegal who has demonstrated mastery of the material through successful completion of a battery of tests.

There are advantages to this model of certification beyond the convenience of a Web-based program. Paralegals no longer have to wait several months to seek advanced certification, and the clearly defined subject matter in a curriculum-based program makes sense to employers.

This curriculum-based model of advanced certification for paralegals may be new to the legal profession, but it is a well-established approach for certification in many other professions. It lends itself well to the NALA program because those who achieve this certification already have the Certified Paralegal credential; they have already demonstrated that they meet the standards of general knowledge and skills required of all paralegals. The new advanced curriculum-based certification is a boon to paralegals wanting recognition of their advanced knowledge and experience, and it is advantageous to employers seeking ways to further develop and train employees.

Courses for the advanced curricula are written by experts in training and development programs and in sequential learning. Similar to the Certified Paralegal program, course writers are guided by an outline developed by a board of experienced paralegals, paralegal educators, attorneys, and paralegal managers. The new programs meet the same high standards of certification and educational programs long sponsored by NALA. They may be relied on by employers and paralegals alike.

The Advanced Paralegal Certification program is ever-changing. For details about the programs and certifications awarded, visit the NALA Web site at http://www.nala.org.

TAKING THE CERTIFIED PARALEGAL EXAMINATION

WHEN

The Certified Paralegal Examination is offered on the following schedule:

Examination Window	Application Filing Deadline**	Late Application Filing Deadline (With $25 late filing fee)
January 1–31	December 1	December 10
May 1–31	April 1	April 10
September 1–30	August 1	August 10

FEES

In 2013, the fee for the Certified Paralegal Examination is $250 for NALA members and $275 for nonmembers. Retake fees are $60 per section. Fees are subject to change at any time.

Examinees must also pay testing center fees. The 2013 PSI testing center fees are as follows. The PSI appointment fees are separate from the examination fees and are paid directly to PSI by the examinee. Payment is required in advance.

- 1.5-hour session—$40
  - 30 minutes for check-in and instructions + 1 hour for the Ethics and Legal Research exams
- 2-hour session—$40
  - 30 minutes for check-in and instructions + 1½ hours for the Communications exam
- 2.5-hour session—$47
  - 30 minutes for check-in and instructions + 2 hours for the Substantive Law or Judgment and Analytical Ability exam

The time stated is the time an examinee will be in attendance at a testing center. Examinees are required to be present 30 minutes in advance to the stated exam start time for check-in and sign-in into the exam session. The PSI testing fees are subject to change at any time.

Examinees may also make arrangements to take an examination at a non-PSI testing center or through their employer. Fees will vary with these arrangements but are generally lower.

APPLICATION APPROVAL AND ADMISSION TO TESTING

Once the application is received and approved, the examinee will receive an acknowledgment of receipt from NALA Headquarters. The acknowledgment may include a request for further information. The application form must be complete upon filing. If the application is rejected because it is incomplete, the fee will be returned, less a $25 processing fee. Shortly before the testing date, the examinee is sent an "authorization to test" form that confirms the testing window, provides an examinee login and password information, and confirms the substantive law areas to be tested. If any of the information is incorrect, the applicant is asked to advise NALA Headquarters. Most communications are sent via e-mail. Examinees are cautioned to keep NALA Headquarters updated of current e-mail addresses.

TESTING TIMES

The examination sections may be taken any time during a testing window based on the examinee's schedule and testing center availability. Times for each exam section are as follows:

Ethics—1 hour
Communications—1.5 hours
Legal Research—1 hours

Substantive Law—2 hours
Judgment and Analytical Ability—2 hours

   For the computer-based testing, timing of an exam section begins once a candidate has selected the appropriate test section from the examinee screen, and the proctor has entered the appropriate credentials to release the examination. There are no scheduled breaks during the exam. If an unscheduled break is required, the clock will continue to run. Times for examination sections are subject to change at any time.

EXAMINATION STRUCTURE
The exam is composed of objective and essay questions.

Objective Questions
- Each objective question will be provided one at a time. Once the answer is selected, examinees are instructed to click "Next" for the next question.
- Each question may be flagged by placing a checkmark in the box entitled "Mark for Review," which appears below the answer options. The selected answer may be changed on review.
- When all questions are completed, the entire list of questions appears. Examinees may review this list before submitting the test for scoring. Questions marked for review by the examinee will be in bold type and can be easily identified. Examinees may also scroll over the text of any question on the list and open it to review the question and selected the answer.
- When the time has expired, access to the exam will be terminated, and the test will be submitted for scoring. Questions that are not completed will be scored as incorrect answers.

Essay Questions
The Judgment and Analytical Ability exam section consists of an essay question. An essay question may be included on other exam sections as determined by the Certifying Board. The following is a description of how essay questions are presented.

   The essay question requires reading. To assist in answering the essay question, candidates will be provided with a printed copy of the essay question when seated to begin the Judgment and Analytical Ability exam section. If a candidate did not receive the printed copy of the essay question, the proctor should be contacted immediately for the printed copy.

   The printed copy of the essay may also be used to make notes and for ease in reading the question. However, space is provided on the computer to input the answer and the answer *must* be typed in the text box provided on the computer screen in order to be graded. The Grading Committee may consider only answers typewritten on the computer window. Examinees will be required to return to the proctor the printed pages prior to leaving the testing center.

   The text box provided for essay question answers will allow examinees to move around within the box, delete, and add sentences and characters as needed. However, cut and paste, spell-check, and other word-processing functions are disabled for all sections of the Certified Paralegal Examination.

   The space provided on the computer screen to type the answer is a text-only box. Examinees are advised *not* to use any special character keys such as ALT, CTRL, or TAB, or the computer workstation may freeze. Candidates must be sure they have completed the essay answer *before* clicking the "Finished Reviewing Present Score" button. Once clicked, access to the examination will terminate.

   Essay questions are graded by members or former members of the Certifying Board. Examinees are instructed *not* to put their name in the response window.

For further information …
The NALA Web site offers detailed information at www.nala.org under the tab "Certification." The pages include detailed information for examinees, as well as those who are certified. The section information is also available in booklet form (PDF files).

Sections on the Web Site	Provides information about . . .
Certification	This section describes the program administration, examination sections, and provides current numbers of Certified Paralegals and Advanced Certified Paralegals.
Certified Paralegal Exam Description	The section provides more detailed information about the examination sections and what they cover, research behind the examination, and information about the latest job analysis study.
Examinees Handbook	Pages in this section are divided into two parts—the application process and testing center details.
Application Form, General Policies, Exam Results	The application pages provide detailed information about applying for the examination, eligibility requirements, policies related to examinees and retakes, cheating and discipline, and examination results.
Testing Centers and Policies, Examination Questions	Testing center pages describe the procedures for finding locations and confirming appointments for the testing sessions. In addition, the testing center rules and policies are listed here. Screen shots of the login and question screens examinees will see on the day of testing are included.
For Certified Paralegals	Pages in this section are divided into two parts: recertification procedures and disciplinary procedures.
Recertification Requirements	The pages describe the recertification requirements followed by all with the Certified Paralegal credential. Included are descriptions of the types of eligible programs, how to file requests for credit, and notices and appeal for revocation of the Certified Paralegal credential based on failure to meet the CLE requirements.
Disciplinary Procedures	The additional pages under "For Certified Paralegals" describe the disciplinary procedures followed by the Certifying Board if a complaint is filed against a Certified Paralegal.
CP Study Materials	This section lists the study materials available for those preparing for the exam. This is also a good source of information for those participating as leaders of review classes.
Qualifying as a Testing Center	This section provides details for employers, schools, and businesses interested in serving as a testing center for their employees or students.
Advanced Paralegal Certification	The Advanced Paralegal Certification Program is available to all Certified Paralegals. This is a curriculum-based certification procedure delivered entirely through Web-based courses.

The information provided here is current at press time but subject to change anytime.

PART
2

Weekly Study Plans

WEEK ONE: COMMUNICATIONS

LESSON PLAN

- Communications Worksheet (30 minutes)
- Review test answers and use them as a basis for discussion/lecture (students grade own)

COMMUNICATIONS—GENERAL DESCRIPTION

Effective communication skills, both oral and written, are the foundation of the paralegal career field. Paralegals are expected to call upon these skills on a daily basis to perform their duties.

Major subject areas of this section are:

Subtopics:

Grammar, punctuation, and capitalization
Word usage, spelling, and vocabulary
Written correspondence and composition
Verbal communication
Nonverbal communication
Client and witness interview preparation and techniques

SUGGESTED TEXT AND REFERENCES

Hurd, Hollis, J. D., *Writing for Lawyers*, Pittsburgh, Pennsylvania, August 2009, www.booksurge.com

Koerselman-Newman, Virginia, J. D., in cooperation with the National Association of Legal Assistants, Inc., *Certified Paralegal Review Manual: A Practical Guide to CP Exam Preparation*, 4th Ed., 2014, Delmar, Cengage Learning.

National Association of Legal Assistants, Inc., *NALA Manual for Paralegals and Legal Assistants*, 5th Ed., 2010, Delmar, Cengage Learning.

Strunk, William, and White, E. B., *The Elements of Style*, 4th Ed. (or most current), 2000, Allyn & Bacon, a Pearson Education Company, Needham Heights, Massachusetts. (Note: Strunk and White, *The Elements of Style*, is the authority adopted by the NALA Certifying Board for the Communications section.)

Webster's New Collegiate Dictionary, 11th Ed. (or most current), G. & C. Merriam Company, Springfield, Massachusetts.

WEEK ONE: COMMUNICATIONS WORKSHEET

For each of the following sentences, mark "C" in front of those that are punctuated correctly and mark "I" for those that are not punctuated correctly.

1. You may choose either Mary or Paul, but not both.

2. I thought I knew the answer; however, I were wrong.

3. The bailiff asked, if the jurors would need pens and paper.

4. Bill shouted, "Where is my umbrella"?

5. When it rains, I prefer to take a taxi; and it always rains on game day.

For each of the following sentences, mark "C" in front of those that are correct and mark "I" for those that are incorrect.

6. Once stop lights were installed at the intersection, there were less accidents.

7. Mr. Wipple seldom criticized Charles's work.

8. If Joe was selected for the position, he would have told me.

9. The steak tasted like it had been broiled for an hour.

10. None of the partners in our firm is over fifty years old.

11. The judge always carries a little, brown tablet with him.

12. I always know where Ken is standing; I simply look for his silver white hair above the crowd.

13. We must obtain his testimony, since our case is quite tenable without it.

14. Whom do you want to see first?

15. Did Kevin realize the bailiff was nearby when he said, "That guy is a jerk."?

Choose the more correct word in each of the following sentences.

16. Diane will do a professional job (irregardless) (regardless) of her personal views.

17. We (implied) (inferred) from the judge's comments that our client would win the case.

18. After three (months') (months) work, the project finally was completed.

19. Willie (set) (sat) the files carefully into the box.

20. The files have been (lying) (laying) on George's desk for more than two weeks.

21. The (client) (client's) sobbing made it impossible to continue the interview.

22. It is the attorney's responsibility to (advise) (inform) the client not to sign the contract without having it reviewed.

23. Everyone felt (badly) (bad) about missing the orientation session.

24. If I (was) (were) in Chicago, I could not have been in New Orleans at the same time.

25. Mary's attitude (aggravated) (irritated) everyone in the elevator.

The following sentences may contain errors in punctuation, capitalization, grammar, and/or word usage. Select the underlined part that must be changed to correct the sentence. Some sentences are correct, and no sentence contains more than one error. If there is no error, select "e."

26. Be sure <u>to carefully draft</u> the contract to include the <u>precise payment</u> and delivery
                a   b
    <u>provisions; even</u> the smallest error <u>cannot be tolerated</u>. <u>No error</u>.
         c   d   e
    a.
    b.
    c.
    d.
    e.

27. When one sells a parcel of real <u>estate, they should</u> <u>ensure that</u> the purchase price is paid in
                                a   b   c
    full before <u>title is</u> transferred. <u>No error</u>.
             d   e
    a.
    b.
    c.
    d.
    e.

28. By <u>May 15, 2013</u>, <u>state legislatures</u> <u>were to have adopted</u> laws to restrict student loans only to
           a   b   c
    <u>those whom</u> lenders believed could repay them. <u>No error</u>.
        d   e
    a.
    b.
    c.
    d.
    e.

29. Especially <u>for we</u> new <u>members, the</u> <u>president should provide</u> a <u>brief, narrative explanation</u>
             a   b   c   d
    before matters are put to a vote. <u>No error</u>.
                              e
    a.
    b.
    c.
    d.
    e.

30. In <u>places like</u> New York and San <u>Francisco, the</u> reason people <u>are uninterested</u> in wearing hats
         a   b   c
    <u>is because</u> it is so windy. <u>No error</u>.
        d   e
    a.
    b.
    c.
    d.
    e.

31. A <u>defendant who</u> has been charged with <u>homicide likely will</u> want to call <u>his or her lawyer</u>
           a   b   c
before answering <u>any specific questions</u> of the arresting officer. <u>No error</u>.
                            d   e

    a.
    b.
    c.
    d.
    e.

Select the answer that is most correct for each of the following sentences.

32. Immediately after work I drove to the judge's reception.
    a. The sentence contains faulty punctuation.
    b. The sentence contains faulty grammar.
    c. The sentence is verbose.
    d. The sentence is correct.

33. Mary as well as her mother enjoys a good joke.
    a. The sentence contains faulty punctuation.
    b. The sentence contains faulty grammar.
    c. The sentence is verbose.
    d. The sentence is correct.

34. Joe recognized the term "exacerbate", but he could not define it.
    a. The sentence contains faulty punctuation.
    b. The sentence contains faulty grammar.
    c. The sentence is verbose.
    d. The sentence is correct.

35. When Dolores saw me, she began to fidget nervously; and I knew she was lying.
    a. The sentence contains faulty punctuation.
    b. The sentence contains faulty grammar.
    c. The sentence is verbose.
    d. The sentence is correct.

36. The reason I ordered a salad was because I was on a diet.
    a. The sentence contains faulty punctuation.
    b. The sentence contains faulty grammar.
    c. The sentence is verbose.
    d. The sentence is correct.

37. People rarely mention all of the hard work done by us paralegals.
    a. The sentence contains faulty punctuation.
    b. The sentence contains faulty grammar.
    c. The sentence is verbose.
    d. The sentence is correct.

38. The lawyer shouting did not help the witness to remain calm.
    a. The sentence contains faulty punctuation.
    b. The sentence contains faulty grammar.
    c. The sentence is verbose.
    d. The sentence is correct.

39. The president selected him and me to serve on the nominating committee.
    a. The sentence contains faulty punctuation.
    b. The sentence contains faulty grammar.
    c. The sentence is verbose.
    d. The sentence is correct.

40. Everyone says that Louis Armstrong Jr. is the one who will succeed.
    a. The sentence contains faulty punctuation.
    b. The sentence contains faulty grammar.
    c. The sentence is verbose.
    d. The sentence is correct.

Choose the answer that most nearly defines the word in each of the following questions.

41. flout
    a. defy
    b. ferret
    c. revere
    d. flaunt

42. avarice
    a. generosity
    b. malevolence
    c. gluttony
    d. malice

43. surreptitious
    a. suspicious
    b. candid
    c. purported
    d. secret

Match each term in the left column with the most correct definition or synonym from the right column.

44. _____ analogy
45. _____ myopic
46. _____ banal
47. _____ rudimentary
48. _____ timorous
49. _____ sanguine
50. _____ fortuitous
51. _____ ennui
52. _____ mendacity
53. _____ misfeasance
54. _____ ultra vires
55. _____ surreptitious

a. basic
b. peevish
c. ignorant
d. example
e. trite
f. carnal
g. short-sighted
h. noisy
i. without authority
j. mousy
k. accidental
l. cheerful
m. secret
n. stubborn
o. lies
p. weariness
q. wrongful performance of lawful act

INTERVIEWING QUIZ

Choose the most correct answer unless you are instructed to do otherwise.

1. True or False. A field interview is conducted only in a wide-open space, free from environmental interference, so the person being interviewed is not distracted.

2. Human relations skills are measured by
   a. one's ability to process the work with the greatest degree of efficiency.
   b. one's ability to work with several individuals in a positive manner.
   c. one's ability to observe ethics rules to the letter.
   d. one's ability to avoid office politics and to ignore the office grapevine.

3. True or False. Understanding the political structure of your law firm is desirable if it becomes necessary to effect change.

4. True or False. It is not necessary for the client to know whom the lawyer or paralegal will interview to obtain additional facts.

5. A hostile witness is
   a. a person who is reluctant to reveal information.
   b. not necessarily one who exhibits hostility.
   c. a witness who displays personal distaste for the client or for the interviewer.
   d. all of the above
   e. none of the above

6. Using technical legal terms during a client interview
   a. is encouraged so the client is assured the lawyer and the paralegal are well educated and knowledgeable.
   b. is appropriate so the client gains familiarity with the legal terminology that will be used in depositions and in court.
   c. should be avoided.
   d. should be explained so the client understands.

7. Empathy is demonstrated when the interviewer
   a. visualizes the situation as the client describes it.
   b. feels what the client feels.
   c. is able to express the client's feelings in objective terms.
   d. all of the above
   e. none of the above

8. True or False. A fact is an event within the personal knowledge of the client or witness.

9. True or False. When a witness knows only a few facts and fills the gaps with information he or she believes the interviewer wishes to hear, the process is called confabulation.

10. True or False. An illustration of a closed question is "Your daughter is not dating Wiley Coyote, is she?"

11. While working with the client, it is
    a. not advisable to share authority with the client during the decision-making process.
    b. best not to let the client become too involved in the fact-gathering process.
    c. basic to the client's understanding to describe the legal process at the outset of the engagement.
    d. best to be selective with the correspondence, documents, and pleadings that are mailed to the client.

12. True or False. If the paralegal is requested by the client not to share specific information with the lawyer, the paralegal has an obligation to the client to keep the information confidential between them.

13. Seating arrangements
    a. are unimportant during an interview.
    b. should be considered because the more comfortable a person is, the more difficulty there is in controlling the direction of the interview.
    c. need be considered only if the person being interviewed is shy.
    d. can help build trust and confidence of those being interviewed.

14. A successful interview requires
    a. planning.
    b. effective use of equipment and resources.
    c. superior human relations skills of the interviewer.
    d. all of the above
    e. b and c only

15. True or False. Open questions produce narrative answers that include factual details known by the person being interviewed.

16. True or False. A question too tactfully framed can produce an evasive answer.

17. A successful interviewer
    a. adapts the communication style of the person being interviewed to his or her style so everyone is talking the "same language."
    b. imitates the communication of the client or witness.
    c. phrases questions simply and clearly.
    d. uses leading questions primarily to seek the information wanted.
    e. all of the above
    f. b and c only
    g. a and d only

18. Corroboration
    a. is the process used to substantiate or to verify the accuracy of an event.
    b. assures the credibility of the client or the witness.
    c. provides supporting evidence for trial.
    d. all of the above
    e. a and c only

19. True or False. The process of verifying facts and details with the client or the witness during the interview is called internal verification.

20. The purpose of the witness statement is to
   a. record the witness's recollection in words more sophisticated and understandable than the witness may be able to communicate for himself or herself.
   b. record the witness's recollection of the events in question.
   c. be letter perfect with the expectation that it will be entered into evidence at trial.
   d. record the names and addresses of other witnesses present.

Match each term in the left column with the most correct definition or synonym from the right column.

21. _____ ad damnum

22. _____ vicissitudes

23. _____ dilettante

24. _____ obviate

25. _____ bane

26. _____ a fortiori

27. _____ nuncupative

28. _____ sui generis

29. _____ nefarious

30. _____ tenancy by the entirety

a. changing fortunes
b. prevent
c. causing drowsiness
d. an amateur, a dabbler
e. inclined to silence
f. affliction; plight
g. to the damage
h. timid, shy
i. husband and wife
j. with greater force
k. criminal, sinister
l. verbal
m. unique, one of a kind
n. lies
o. noisy

ANSWERS TO WEEK ONE: COMMUNICATIONS WORKSHEET

1. C—also correct without the comma
2. C—directions say to correct for punctuation, not grammar
3. I—no comma needed
4. I—question mark inside quote
5. C
6. I—wrong word, should be *fewer* instead of *less*
7. C
8. I—*were* instead of *was*
9. I—*as if* or *as though* instead of *like*
10. C
11. C—comma required because of compound adjective
12. C—not the best style, but sentence contains no errors
13. I—wrong word—*tenable* should be *tenuous*
14. C—You want to see *him* first, so *whom* is correct.
15. I—delete the period; otherwise, ok
16. regardless
17. inferred
18. months'
19. set
20. lying
21. client's
22. advise
23. bad (no need to "dress up")
24. was (fact)
25. irritated
26. a—split infinitive
27. b—pronoun must agree with antecedent
28. d—who (used as subject of clause who could repay them)
29. a—us (object of preposition)
30. d—reason is because (redundant, verbose)
31. e
32. a—comma after *work*
33. d—no comma with *as well as*
34. a—comma inside quote
35. d
36. c—reason is because = redundant
37. d
38. a—should be *lawyer's*
39. d
40. d
41. a
42. c
43. d
44. d
45. g
46. e
47. a
48. j

49. l
50. k
51. p
52. o
53. q
54. i
55. m

ANSWERS TO INTERVIEWING QUIZ

1.	False	16.	True
2.	b	17.	f
3.	True	18.	d
4.	False	19.	True
5.	d	20.	b
6.	c	21.	g
7.	d	22.	a
8.	True	23.	d
9.	True	24.	b
10.	False	25.	f
11.	c	26.	j
12.	False	27.	l
13.	d	28.	m
14.	d	29.	k
15.	True	30.	i

WEEK TWO:
JUDGMENT AND ANALYTICAL ABILITY

LESSON PLAN

- Communications Worksheet (10 minutes); go over answers; students grade own
- Judgment Quiz (30 minutes); go over answers; students grade own
- Judgment Essay (30 minutes; students prepare outline only for answers); go over in class

JUDGMENT AND ANALYTICAL ABILITY—GENERAL DESCRIPTION

Paralegals must be able to analyze a problem, relate it to case law and legal precedents, and compose documents that summarize their analysis and findings. The examination consists of an assignment from a supervising attorney in which the applicant is provided with a fact situation and supporting statutory and case law. Applicants must analyze the problem and additional materials, and prepare a summary of their findings and analysis as directed. The following judgment and analytical skills are tested:

Identification of relevant facts and main issues
Application of law to facts
Analysis of issues and formation of conclusions
Organization of information and clarity of expression

SUGGESTED TEXT AND REFERENCES

Judgment and Analytical Ability

Currier, Katherine, and Eimermann, Thomas, Ph.D., *Introduction to Paralegal Studies: A Critical Thinking Approach*, 4th Ed., 2009, Aspen Publishers.

Koerselman-Newman, Virginia, J. D., in cooperation with the National Association of Legal Assistants, Inc., *Certified Paralegal Review Manual: A Practical Guide to CP Exam Preparation*, 4th Ed., 2014, Delmar, Cengage Learning.

National Association of Legal Assistants, Inc., *NALA Manual for Paralegals and Legal Assistants*, 5th Ed., 2010, Delmar, Cengage Learning.

Rombauer, Marjorie Dick, *Legal Problem Solving: Analysis, Research & Writing*, 5th Ed., 1991, Delmar, Cengage Learning.

WEEK TWO: COMMUNICATIONS WORKSHEET

Make corrections as necessary to the following sentences. Write "C" in front of those sentences that are correct as written.

1. We will probably be sorry that we did not start sooner.

2. To ignore the problem is like saying that we don't care.

3. After debating the issue for a week yet they did not come to an agreement, the committee members gave up in disgust.

4. I believe the classes have been fairly effective, but we can improve it.

5. Some favorite winter activities are skiing, tobogganing, and to sit by the fire.

6. The plane's landing gear banged against the pavement, but it was not damaged.

7. Two players were knocked out on the play but not being seriously injured.

8. I would have liked to have been in competitive sports when I was young.

9. Jan worries from the time she gets up until she goes to bed about many things.

10. Half of the citizens cannot understand the Constitution in this country.

11. To pay my bills, I only need to work part time.

12. I didn't do near as well as him on the test.

13. A tighter system of controls will always be needed.

14. If the legal drinking age was lower, it would lead to more auto accidents.

15. If Angela was with you, I am certain that she enjoyed her tour.

16. Raymond felt boldly enough to ask Martha to dinner.

17. Six dollars is a great deal of money for such a small unnecessary book.

18. Jack found a part time job.

19. The rights of people that use guns for sport should be protected.

JUDGMENT AND ANALYTICAL ABILITY QUIZ

For each of the following sentences, select the answer that is most correct.

20. If the court ruled against our client sua sponte,
    a. the court itself made the required motion.
    b. the court's ruling was made spontaneously, or "on the spot."
    c. the court took the ruling under advisement.
    d. the court ruled without citing any case or statute as its basis.

21. A contract is executed when it is
    a. signed.
    b. performed.
    c. breached.
    d. litigated.

Following the paragraph set out below are questions based on its contents. After reading the paragraph, select the best answer for each question. Base your answers to the questions only on what is stated or implied in the paragraph.

> *The burden of proof is the standard that the fact finder is to apply to a set of facts in determining how to reach a verdict. A preponderance of the evidence must be shown for the plaintiff to prevail in a civil case. This is interpreted to mean that the plaintiff's version of the facts is correct rather than the defendant's version of the facts. In the charge to the jury by the trial judge, the applicable burden of proof is always covered. In civil cases, the jurors frequently are asked to imagine a set of scales with the plaintiff's evidence on one side and the defendant's evidence on the other. If the equilibrium of the scale is perfect or if the defendant's scale is lower than the plaintiff's, plaintiff may not recover since the burden of proof has not been satisfied. If the plaintiff's scale of evidence is heavier than the defendant's scale of evidence so that it goes lower, no matter how much lower, plaintiff is entitled to recover.*

22. Which of the following expresses the best title for this paragraph?
    a. The Balancing of the Legal Scales
    b. The Plaintiff's Side v. the Defendant's Side
    c. The Burden of Proof
    d. How a Jury Determines Facts

23. Which statement is false according to the paragraph?
    a. Jurors are sometimes asked to use their imaginations when it comes to questions of evidence.
    b. Plaintiff may recover if the defendant's scales are lower.
    c. A preponderance of the evidence must be shown for the plaintiff to prevail in a civil case.
    d. If the plaintiff's scale of evidence is heavier than the defendant's scale, the plaintiff is entitled to recover.

24. One may conclude most correctly from the paragraph that
    a. in applying the burden of proof to a set of facts in reaching a verdict, the plaintiff must show a heavier weight of evidence.
    b. in charging the jury, the judge generally covers the applicable burden of proof.
    c. equilibrium of the scales of justice is evenly balanced when presenting evidence to the jury.
    d. a lot of imagination is used by jurors in deciding the burden of proof based on evidence.

For each of the following situations, select the answer that is most correct.

25. Paralegals in your firm are assigned to work with specific teams of attorneys. Although you have been suspicious for some time, it now is clear to you that the senior attorney on your team is charging some of his clients for more time than was used to do the work. Your best course of action is to
    a. bring the situation to the attention to another attorney of equal or greater seniority whom you trust.
    b. delete the extra hours from the clients' billings and keep the correction to yourself.
    c. keep the situation to yourself and start looking for different employment.
    d. contact the client to see how he or she feels about the matter.

26. Jay is an experienced paralegal with the firm Arnold & Stone. Jay received a telephone call from a client in which the client told Jay she was sending a duplicate of the contract that Mr. Stone said Jay had lost. Since Jay was certain that the attorney, not he, had lost the contract copy, Jay was livid. What is Jay's best course of action?
    a. Inform the client that he (Jay) did not lose the contract copy.
    b. Say nothing to the client, but confront Mr. Stone about the misrepresentation.
    c. Apologize to the client and say nothing to Mr. Stone.
    d. Apologize to the client and inform Mr. Stone of what the client related.

27. Regina, a paralegal with 12 years' experience, is interviewing for a position with a large law firm. She has wanted to work with this firm for at least 2 years. After discussing Regina's background and the requirements of the job, the interviewer asked Regina whether she planned to have children. Which of the following responses is best under the circumstances?
    a. "How should I know?"
    b. "You can't ask me that. It is against the law."
    c. "If I do, it will not interfere with my career."
    d. "I do not plan to have children in the foreseeable future."

28. In the same circumstances described in the preceding question, which would be the worst response from among those listed?
    a. "How should I know?"
    b. "You can't ask me that. It is against the law."
    c. "If I do, it will not interfere with my career."
    d. "I do not plan to have children in the foreseeable future."

29. You are a paralegal for a collections attorney. One afternoon while the attorney is away, a woman appears in the office. You recognize her as your neighbor, although you had not known her last name previously. She recognizes you as well and begins to cry. Apparently, her employer had just been served with a garnishment of her wages. Your office represents the judgment creditor.
    You know that she is a single mother with nine children, that she has financial problems, and that she is struggling to support her family. She begs you to help her, since she does not have enough money left to buy food for her children this week. She asks if there is anything she can do. Her distress is genuine, and she seems completely helpless. Your employer will not be back in the office until Monday of next week. By that time, the employer will have forwarded the garnished wages to the court. Select the best course of action.
    a. Find out if she has a lawyer; if not, offer to call the creditor for her.
    b. Find out if she has a lawyer; if not, tell her to call the creditor herself and tell her what to say.
    c. Call your employer and find out what she wants you to do.
    d. Tactfully tell her there is nothing you can do.

30. The law clerk in your office is assigned to work with you on a particular litigation case. The two of you are to review certain client documents in anticipation of discovery disclosure and requests. The law clerk discovers several pages of handwritten notes that are extremely damaging to the client's case. He removes the pages, declaring that they must have been left in the file by mistake. Your best course of action is to
    a. notify the supervising attorney and let her determine what to do.
    b. call the bar association and find out if you can remove the pages.
    c. discuss your reservation with the law clerk and have him call the bar association.
    d. discuss your reservation with the law clerk and have him check with the supervising attorney concerning propriety.

31. In the same situation as the preceding question, you later discover the handwritten pages in the wastebasket. The law clerk maintains that since the pages were erroneously placed in the file, there can be no basis for requiring them to be left there. Which is your best course of action?
    a. Tell the law clerk that he will be fired immediately.
    b. Call the bar association and find out if you can remove the pages.
    c. Notify the supervising attorney and let her determine what to do.
    d. Remind the law clerk that he promised to check with the supervising attorney.

32. To work most effectively, a paralegal must
    a. know who directs his or her work.
    b. know whose work, if any, he or she directs.
    c. neither is correct
    d. both are correct

33. True or False. One way for a new paralegal to gain the respect of others in the law office or law department is to look for antiquated systems and practices and to push for their immediate modification.

34. True or False. If a system works well in one law firm, one reasonably may assume that the system will work well in another law firm with the same number of lawyers.

35. True or False. If a paralegal is instructed by the supervising attorney to obtain a special type of marking pencil to prepare a special exhibit for trial, it is not reasonable to assume that the paralegal has authority to charge the exhibit tabs to the firm's account at the office supply store.

36. Linda is a new paralegal at Garcia & Hicks. She notices at once that most of the paralegals answer their own telephone and do their own filing. Which of the following assumptions can be made in this circumstance?
    a. The firm does not know how to use paralegals properly.
    b. Management believes this to be the most efficient way to handle the work.
    c. The paralegals are being used as glorified secretaries.
    d. Both a and c are true.
    e. None of the above is true.

37. You are an experienced paralegal. Your supervising attorney has assigned to you the task of creating a control plan to catalog and summarize a room full of client documents in preparation for litigation. The litigation will be filed in approximately 4 weeks. Clearly, this will be a monumental job. Your best course of action at this point is to
    a. review one or two of the boxes of documents, complete the tasks assigned, keep track of the time required, and review the project with your supervisor to determine how much time and how many people will be required to complete the assignment.
    b. formulate the control plan, review it with your supervisor, and then implement the plan.
    c. find out who may be available to assist you since you obviously cannot complete such a large project in so little time, and work with that individual in formulating and implementing the control plan.
    d. discreetly let your friends in other offices know that you are looking for a new job.

For each of the following situations, select the answer that is most correct.

38. Two is to six as _____ is to _____.
    a. 6 : 2
    b. 3 : 1
    c. 7 : 21
    d. 7 : 49

39. Herd is to cows as _____ is to _____.
    a. alphabet : letters
    b. garage : cars
    c. wheel : spokes
    d. barn : horses

40. Business is to manager as _____ is to _____.
    a. president : country
    b. government : business
    c. Senate : Congress
    d. city : mayor

EXERCISE NO. 5: MEMORANDUM

TO: Janet Barnes, Paralegal

DATE: (today's date)

FROM: Virginia Koerselman, Staff Attorney

RE: Dan Sampson
           New Client File

Dan Sampson is an 18-year-old construction worker who lives with his parents. Shortly after he was employed, he bought a car. His father co-signed for the loan. Then Dan bought a $600 television set for his room. After the warranty had expired on the television set, it stopped working. Dan took the set to Easy Eddie's Repair Shop to be fixed. When Dan left the television, Farley, the head bookkeeper at Easy Eddie's, required Dan to sign an agreement authorizing the repair shop to make whatever repairs might be necessary and obligating Dan to pay for any necessary repairs that were made. Eddie promised the television set would be ready to pick up by the end of the week.

On that Friday, Dan appeared at the repair shop to pick up his television set. It was not ready. Dan stopped on the following Friday as well as the Friday after that. Dan became very upset at being put off and demanded that the television set be returned to him at once. After a long discussion, Eddie, the owner, convinced Dan to leave the set and promised that it would be ready the following Wednesday.

On Wednesday, Dan came to the repair shop and learned that the set had been repaired. Eddie presented him with the repair invoice for $607.35. Dan became very upset that the shop would spend more to repair the set than the set had cost originally. Eddie reminded Dan that he had signed a contract to pay for necessary repairs and told him to "take it or leave it." Dan was incensed. He stomped out of the shop without paying the invoice and without his television set.

After brooding about the matter for several days, Dan and one of his friends parked near the repair shop on the following Friday. Dan knew that the shop was busy on Fridays; and while all of the clerks were helping customers, Dan slipped into the backroom. He found his set, took it out the backdoor, and put it in his friend's car. Dan and his friend then drove away.

On the following day, two police officers appeared at Dan's home with a search warrant. Dan's mother let them in the house. They found the television and arrested Dan for theft. He was released on his own recognizance. Dan's parents, Joe and Betty Sampson, are longtime clients and have retained our firm to represent their son.

The following statutes may apply to this case. Prepare a memorandum to me concerning Dan's potential criminal and civil liability based on these statutory provisions.

Use proper memorandum form that includes facts, issue(s), discussion, and conclusion.

Statutes
§ 28-507.   Burglary; penalty.

(1) A person commits burglary if such person willfully, maliciously, and forcibly breaks and enters any real estate or any improvements erected thereon with intent to commit any felony or with intent to steal property of any value.
(2) Burglary is a Class III felony.

§ 28-511.   Theft by unlawful taking or disposition.

(1) A person is guilty of theft if he or she takes, or exercises control over, movable property of another with the intent to deprive him or her thereof.
(2) A person is guilty of theft if he or she transfers immovable property of another or any interest therein with the intent to benefit himself or herself or another not entitled thereto.

§ 28-512.   Theft by deception.
A person commits theft if he or she obtains property of another by deception. A person deceives if he intentionally:

(1) Creates or reinforces a false impression, including false impressions as to law, value, intent, or other state of mind; but deception as to a person's intent to perform a promise shall not be inferred from the fact alone that he or she subsequently did not perform the promise; or
(2) Prevents another from acquiring information which would affect his judgment of a transaction; or
(3) Fails to correct a false impression which the deceiver previously created or reinforced, or which the deceiver knows to be influencing another to whom he stands in a fiduciary or confidential relationship.

§ 28-518.   Grading of theft offenses.

(1) Theft constitutes a Class III felony when the value of the thing involved is over one thousand dollars.
(2) Theft constitutes a Class IV felony when the value of the thing involved is three hundred dollars or more, but not over one thousand dollars.
(3) Theft constitutes a Class I misdemeanor when the value of the thing involved is more than one hundred dollars, but less than three hundred dollars.

§ 43-2101.   Persons declared minors; effect.
All persons under nineteen years of age are declared to be minors, but in case any such person marries under the age of nineteen years, his or her minority ends. The contracts of persons who are minors may be declared void, at the option of such minor person, during his or her minority or within a reasonable time after his or her minority ends.

§ 52-202.   Artisan's lien.
Any person who makes, alters, repairs, or in any way enhances the value of any vehicle, automobile, machinery, appliance, implement, or tool at the request of or with the consent of the owner or owners thereof, shall have a lien upon such vehicle, automobile, machinery, appliance, implement, or tool while in his possession, for the reasonable or agreed charges for the work done or material furnished, and shall have the right to retain such property until such charges are paid.

ANSWERS TO WEEK TWO: COMMUNICATIONS WORKSHEET

1. split verb—We probably will be sorry that we did not start sooner.
2. To ignore the problem is saying that we don't care.
    Suggest: To ignore . . . is to say . . .
                 Ignoring is saying . . .
                 Ignoring the problem says . . .
3. After debating the issue for a week without coming to an agreement, the committee members gave up in disgust.
4. pronoun agreement with antecedent—I believe the classes have been fairly effective, but we can improve them.
5. parallel construction—Some favorite winter activities are skiing, tobogganing, and sitting by the fire.
6. what was not damaged? The plane's landing gear banged against the pavement, but it (the landing gear? the pavement?) was not damaged.
7. parallel construction—Two players were knocked out on the play but were not seriously injured.
8. tense of the infinitive—I would have liked to have been in competitive sports when I was young.
    now = I would like to have been (then)
    back then = I would have liked to be (at that time)
9. misplaced modifier—Jan worries about many things from the time she gets up until she goes to bed.
10. misplaced modifier—Half of the citizens in this country cannot understand the Constitution.
11. misplaced modifier—To pay my bills, I need to work only part time.
12. I didn't do nearly as well as he (did) on the test.
13. split verb—A tighter system of controls always will be needed.
14. subjunctive mood—conditional *if*—If the legal drinking age were lower, it would lead to more auto accidents.
15. C
16. subject complement; the adjective form describes Raymond—Raymond felt bold enough to ask Martha to dinner.
17. add a comma—compound adjective—Six dollars is a great deal of money for such a small, unnecessary book.
18. add a hyphen—Jack found a part-time job.
19. The rights of people who use guns for sport should be protected.

ANSWERS TO JUDGMENT AND ANALYTICAL ABILITY QUIZ

20.	a	31.	c
21.	b	32.	d
22.	c	33.	False
23.	b	34.	False
24.	a	35.	True
25.	a	36.	b
26.	d	37.	a
27.	c	38.	c
28.	b	39.	a
29.	d	40.	d
30.	d		

ANSWER TO EXERCISE NO. 5: MEMORANDUM

Outline for Answer

Issue(s):

1. What is client's potential criminal liability?
   - Artisan's lien of $607.35 to Easy Eddie if TV is "appliance" 52-202
     —TV probably is appliance
   - Theft by unlawful taking 28-511(1)
     —control of property of another (via lien) with intent to deprive
     —not burglary = no forcible breaking or forcible entering 28-507
     —not theft by deception = no deception—just took TV outright 28-512
   - Class IV felony = more than $300 but less than $1,000 28-518(2)

2. What is client's potential civil liability?
   - Artisan's lien in favor of Easy Eddie for $607.35 52-202
     —foreclose lien by selling TV for fair market value
   - Return TV to lien holder or pay repair charges
     —perhaps dispute necessity of repairs but need factual basis

Relevant Facts:

- Dan Sampson is client
- Bought TV for $600
- TV stopped working after warranty expired
- Took TV to Easy Eddie's Repair Shop and signed contract for necessary repairs
- After delays, TV was repaired at cost of $607.35
- Client refused to pay more than TV was worth and left
- Returned on following Friday and, while clerks were busy with customers, slipped into the backroom and took his TV home
- Arrested by police and released on his own recognizance

Sample Answer

MEMORANDUM

TO: Virginia Koerselman, Staff Attorney

DATE: (today's date)

FROM: Janet Barnes, Paralegal

RE: Dan Sampson
         New Client File

You have asked me to review specific statutes to determine Dan Sampson's civil and criminal liability, if any, concerning events surrounding repair of his television set by Easy Eddie's Repair Shop.

Facts:

We represent Dan Sampson, an 18-year-old construction worker who bought a television set for $600. After the warranty expired, the television set stopped working. Dan took the set to Easy Eddie's Repair Shop and signed a contract under the terms of which he agreed to pay for any repairs necessary to fix the television.

After several delays, the repairs were completed at a cost of $607.35. Dan refused to pay the invoice because the amount was more than he had paid for the television originally. He left the repair shop without the television set.

Dan and one of his friends returned to the repair shop several days later. While all of the clerks were busy with customers, Dan slipped into the backroom and took his television out the backdoor. He was arrested the next day with the television in his possession. Subsequently, he was released on his own recognizance.

Issues:

1. What is Dan's potential criminal liability in taking the television from Easy Eddie's Repair Shop without paying for it?
2. What is Dan's potential civil liability in taking the television from Easy Eddie's Repair Shop without paying for it?

Discussion:

If a television is an appliance (and it probably is), the repair shop appears to have a valid artisan's lien under § 52-202 since it repaired the television at the request or with the consent of our client. Accordingly, the repair shop was entitled to possession of the television until the amount of its lien was paid.

Dan most likely violated § 28-511(1) when he removed the television set from the shop without paying for the repairs. Under this statute, a person is guilty of theft by unlawful taking if he or she "exercises control over movable property of another with the intent to deprive him or her thereof." Although the repair shop did not own the television set, it did have the right to possess it based upon its artisan's lien. Dan violated that possessory right when he took the television from the shop without paying for its repair. Since Dan did not enter the shop forcibly and did not deceive anyone, he does not appear to have violated the statutes prohibiting burglary or theft by deception, respectively.

Theft by unlawful taking under § 28-511(1) will be graded as a Class IV felony in this case if the property is valued between $300 and $1,000, as appears to be the case. § 28-518(2). If the fair market value of the television is less than $300, it is a Class I misdemeanor. § 28-518(3).

Dan's potential civil liability is tied to the validity of the artisan's lien created by repair of his television set at his request or with his consent under § 52-202. Dan signed a contract agreeing to pay for necessary repairs. Even if this contract could be avoided based on Dan's minority, the repair shop still would be entitled to the reasonable value of its repair work, which may leave Dan in no better position than he is in now.

It may be possible to dispute the necessity of the repairs or to dispute the reasonableness of their cost; however, we currently have no facts upon which to base claims such as these. Without such a factual basis, Dan's best interests may be served by paying the repair cost. This course of action cancels any potential civil liability and may go far in persuading the prosecutor and the repair shop to drop any criminal charges.

Conclusion:

Because of the repair shop's artisan's lien on the television set owned by Dan Sampson, Dan most likely committed theft by unlawful taking when he removed the set from the repair shop. This may be either a Class IV felony or a Class I misdemeanor depending on the fair market value of the television set when it was taken.

Dan's civil liability to the repair shop is the reasonable value of the repairs made to his television set. Unless Dan pays this cost, he will be obligated to return the television set to Easy Eddie's Repair Shop so that Eddie may foreclose his lien by selling the property. Considering all known facts, Dan's best course of action may be simply to pay the repair charges.

WEEK THREE:
LEGAL RESEARCH

LESSON PLAN

- Communications Worksheet (10 minutes); go over answers; students grade own
- Legal Research Quiz (30 minutes); go over answers; students grade own
- Show students how to set up their own timeline/chart to study details of legal research

LEGAL RESEARCH—GENERAL DESCRIPTION

Paralegals must be able to use the most important tool of the legal profession, the law library. The purpose of this section of the Certified Paralegal Examination is to test one's knowledge of the use of state and federal codes, statutes, digests, case reports, various legal encyclopedias, court reports, and research procedures.

Major subject areas of this section are:

Sources of law
Research skills
Analysis of research

SUGGESTED TEXT AND REFERENCES

Berring, Robert C., and Edinger, Elizabeth, *Berring and Edinger's Finding the Law*, 12th Ed., 2005, Thomson Reuters Westlaw.

Cohen, Morris L., and Olson, Kent, *Cohen and Olson's Legal Research in a Nutshell*, 10th Ed. (or most current), 2010, Thomson Reuters Westlaw.

Koerselman-Newman, Virginia, J. D., in cooperation with the National Association of Legal Assistants, Inc., *Certified Paralegal Review Manual: A Practical Guide to CP Exam Preparation*, 4th Ed., 2014, Delmar, Cengage Learning.

Shepard's Citations Service, Lexisnexis, www.lexisnexis.com

A Uniform System of Citation, 19th Ed., Harvard Law Review Association. (Note: *A Uniform System of Citation* is the authority adopted by the NALA Certifying Board for the Legal Research section.)

WEEK THREE: COMMUNICATIONS WORKSHEET

Make corrections as necessary to the following sentences. Write "C" in front of those sentences that are correct as written.

1. Paralegals must be familiar with Westlaw and Lexis-Nexis to better use their time devoted to legal research.

2. I shall have worked many hours by the time this project is finished.

3. Bill shall have worked many hours as well.

4. I had trouble knowing what to do about it at first.

5. Neither Sam nor his sons has attended college.

6. The campaign headquarters are located near our office building.

7. Everyone on our block had their mailboxes stolen.

8. You have more challenge in your job than me.

9. I don't care who the chairperson chooses.

10. There is a fine piano for sale by an elderly woman with carved legs.

11. We need to carefully plan our course of action.

12. Judy worked like a crazed woman.

13. Although the motorcycle hit the abutment with considerable force, it was not damaged.

14. A student never should cheat; even if you don't get caught, you will do great harm to yourself.

15. The judge's decision broke a hundred year old precedent.

16. Above the buzzards circled ominously.

17. The Wright Brothers' unique creative achievement led to the supersonic jets that now scream through the skies.

For the next group of questions, match each term in the left column with the word or phrase in the right column that most accurately defines or describes it.

18. _____ extrapolate	a.	deduce
19. _____ ab initio	b.	affirming existence; empirical
	c.	that is to say, namely
20. _____ elucidate	d.	and husband
21. _____ temerity	e.	pledge as security for debt
22. _____ refractory	f.	and others
23. _____ extricate	g.	illogical, does not follow
	h.	disengage
24. _____ existential	i.	clarify
25. _____ et vir	j.	from the beginning
26. _____ et al.	k.	audacity
	l.	notwithstanding
27. _____ hypothecate	m.	unjust, unfair
28. _____ non sequitur	n.	unmanageable

LEGAL RESEARCH QUIZ

Select the best answer for each of the following questions unless a specific question instructs you to do otherwise.

1. True or False. *Statutes at Large* is an official publication that includes all laws enacted by Congress.

2. True or False. *The United States Code* is an official publication that includes all laws enacted by Congress.

3. True or False. Each state publishes an official reporter that includes decisions of its highest state court.

4. True or False. *The Federal Supplement* includes all decisions of the United States District Courts across the country.

5. True or False. *The Federal Supplement* is an official reporter.

6. True or False. *The Federal Reporter*, Second Series, includes all decisions of the United States Courts of Appeals across the country.

7. True or False. *The Federal Reporter*, Second Series, is an official reporter.

8. True or False. The terms *memorandum opinion* and *memorandum of law* mean approximately the same thing.

9. True or False. Statutes are published as session laws before they are codified.

10. True or False. The American Digest System includes the Decennial Digests and a General Digest.

11. Federal session laws may be found in
    a. the *Federal Register*.
    b. the *Federal Reporter*.
    c. *Statutes at Large*.
    d. *United States Code*.

12. *U.S. Law Week*
    a. is an official publication.
    b. contains recent decisions of the U.S. Supreme Court.
    c. contains recent decisions of all federal appellate courts.
    d. all of the above

13. The official reporter of the U.S. Supreme Court is
    a. *United States Reports*.
    b. *Supreme Court Reporter*.
    c. *Supreme Court Reporter*, Lawyers Edition.
    d. none of the above

14. *Obiter dictum* is a Latin term that refers to the
    a. overall decision of a court case.
    b. holding of a court case.
    c. court's explanation of the holding in the case.
    d. court's comments about things other than the holding in the case.

15. The record of a court case includes
    a. pleadings, transcript of trial testimony, and exhibits.
    b. pleadings, briefs, motions, transcript of trial testimony, and exhibits.
    c. transcript of trial testimony and exhibits.
    d. all documents filed in the trial court.

16. When an appellate court reviews a case *de novo* on the record, it
    a. tries the case anew, as if no trial had occurred in the lower court.
    b. reviews the record only for errors of law committed by the trial court.
    c. reviews the record for errors of law and reaches its own factual finding.
    d. none of the above

17. Until 1932, cases from the U.S. Court of Appeals and the U.S. District Court were combined in
    a. Federal Cases.
    b. the *Federal Reporter*.
    c. the *Federal Supplement*.
    d. none of the above

18. Star paging is
    a. used throughout federal case reporters.
    b. used to refer to the page number of the original reporter when a case is reprinted in another reporter.
    c. used to indicate where the holding of the case appears.
    d. none of the above

19. To update the status of a particular statute, one may use a(n)
    a. digest.
    b. index.
    c. supplement volume or pocket part supplement.
    d. none of the above

20. To determine whether a particular statute has been ruled unconstitutional by a court, one may use
    a. *Shepard's Citations*.
    b. *Shepard's Citations*, Statute Edition.
    c. *Shepard's Citations*, Case Edition.
    d. a supplement to the statutory code.

21. Which of the following represent primary authority?
    a. case law, Constitution, rules of procedure, restatements of law
    b. judicial legislation, rules of procedure, Constitution, statutes
    c. rules of procedure, case law, statutes, Constitution
    d. session laws, case law, annotations, Constitution, legal dictionaries

22. Which of the following provides background information for a research topic?
    a. *Shepard's Citations*
    b. *United States Code Annotated*
    c. *American Jurisprudence Second*
    d. American Digest System

23. Which of the following represent secondary authority?
    a. legal dictionary, treatise, restatement of law, encyclopedia
    b. encyclopedia, digest, legal dictionary, common law
    c. case law from other jurisdictions, common law, treatise, session laws
    d. restatement of law, treatise, slip law, encyclopedia

24. If a researcher knows when a federal statute was enacted, which of the following provides the most direct access to the text of that statute?
    a. *United States Code*
    b. *Code of Federal Regulations*
    c. *Congressional Record*
    d. *U.S. Law Week*

25. When a researcher intends to show that a statement in his or her brief is supported directly by the cited case, the researcher should use which of the following signals with the citation?
    a. see
    b. cf.
    c. accord
    d. no signal is used

For Questions 26–35, assume that you have been assigned to review the form of citation in connection with an appellate brief. Edit the questions as required to show the correct citation form. If the citation is correct as shown, write the word **correct** *immediately before the question number.*

26. *Constitutional Law*, 16 Am.Jur.2d § 349, 213 (1987).

27. *J.C. Penney Co., Inc. v. Mary Staats*, 329 Neb. 464, 617 N.W.2d 456 (1991).

28. *EEOC v. Manning*, 440 U.S. 29, 566 S. Ct. 908, 790 L. Ed. 2d 46 (1983).

29. *IRS v. Richardson*, 156 T.C. 677 (1992).

30. Tax Procurement Act, 39 U.S. Code § 117 (1990).

31. *Kellum v. Riedstrom*, 464 F.2d 366 (5th Cir. 1989).

32. *Kellum, supra*, at 370.

33. *United States v. Claussen*, 613 Fed. Supp. 296 (E.D.N.Y. 1989).

34. *Black's Law Dictionary* 768 (7th ed. 1992).

35. *Davis v. Central R.R. Co., Inc.*, 509 F.2d 199, 201 (8th Cir. 1988).

Choose the most correct answer unless you are instructed to do otherwise.

36. When an appellate judge disagrees with the result and with the reasoning of the majority opinion and disagrees with the reasoning of the dissenting opinion as well, he or she may write a
    a. concurring opinion.
    b. memorandum opinion.
    c. partially dissenting opinion.
    d. dissenting opinion.

37. Briefly explain the difference between the terms *supra* and *infra*.

38. True or False. The *Statutes at Large* is compiled chronologically; the *United States Code* is compiled by topic.

39. True or False. The opinions of federal trial courts are contained in the *Federal Reporter*, Second Series.

40. True or False. When a researcher knows the case citation, the best tool for locating parallel citations for the case is West's *National Reporter Blue Book*.

41. True or False. There is a separate digest to accompany each of the reporters that contain U.S. Supreme Court cases.

42. True or False. A per curiam opinion is a unanimous opinion of the entire court.

43. F.R.D. contains:
    a. rules of Congress.
    b. decisions of administrative agencies concerning their rules and regulations.
    c. decisions concerning federal rules of procedure.
    d. decisions concerning local rules of federal courts.

44. The U.S. Constitution may be found in
    a. each volume of *U.S. Reports*.
    b. the first volume of the *Federal Practice Digest*.
    c. the first volume of the *United States Code*.
    d. none of the above

45. An executive order is classified as
    a. statutory law.
    b. case law.
    c. administrative law.
    d. none of the above

46. A decision of an administrative agency is classified as
    a. statutory law.
    b. case law.
    c. common law.
    d. none of the above

47. True or False. Presidential proclamations are published in the *Statutes at Large*.

48. True or False. *The Federal Supplement* includes selected decisions from the Court of International Trade.

49. True or False. Common law has existed in some form since history first was recorded.

50. True or False. A.L.R. stands for *American Law Reports*.

For the next group of questions, fill in each blank with the term or phrase that best fits the definition shown.

51. _____ previously decided

52. _____ the thing speaks for itself

53. _____ triers of fact

54. _____ a matter adjudicated

55. _____ Latin term meaning "note well"

ANSWERS TO WEEK THREE: COMMUNICATIONS WORKSHEET

1. split infinitive—Paralegals must be familiar with Westlaw and Lexis-Nexis to use their time devoted to legal research **better.**
2. C
3. person of the verb—Bill **will** have worked many hours as well.
4. misplaced modifier—I had trouble at first knowing what to do about it.
5. subject-verb agreement—Neither Sam nor his sons **have** attended college.
6. subject-verb agreement—The campaign headquarters **is** located near our office building.
7. pronoun agreement with antecedent—Everyone on our block had **his or her mailbox** stolen.
8. subjunctive-pronoun case—You have more challenge in your job than **I**.
9. pronoun case—I don't care **whom** the chairperson chooses.
10. misplaced modifier—There is a fine piano **with carved legs** for sale by an elderly woman.
11. split infinitive—We need to plan our course of action **carefully**.
12. C
13. as written, *it* refers to abutment; what is *it?*—Although the motorcycle hit the abutment with considerable force, **it** (what? the cycle? the abutment?) was not damaged.
14. person switched in midsentence—A student never should cheat; even if **she doesn't** get caught, **she** will do great harm to **herself**.
15. compound adjective preceding noun—The judge's decision broke a **hundred-year-old** precedent.
16. add comma—**Above,** the buzzards circled ominously.
    (Also correct: The buzzards circled above ominously.)
    (Also correct: The buzzards circled ominously above.)
17. add comma; compound adjective—The Wright Brothers' **unique, creative** achievement led to the supersonic jets that now scream through the skies.
18. a
19. j
20. i
21. k
22. n
23. h
24. b
25. d
26. f
27. e
28. g

ANSWERS TO LEGAL RESEARCH QUIZ

1. True
2. False
3. False
4. False
5. False
6. False
7. False
8. False
9. True
10. True

11. c
12. b
13. a
14. d
15. a
16. c
17. b
18. b
19. c
20. b
21. c
22. c
23. a
24. c
25. d
26. 16 Am.Jur.2d *Constitutional Law* § 349, 213 (1987).
27. *J.C. Penney Co. v. Staats*, 329 Neb. 464, 617 N.W.2d 456 (1991).
28. *EEOC v. Manning*, 440 U.S. 29 (1983).
29. *Commissioner v. Richardson*, 156 T.C. 677 (1992).
30. Tax Procurement Act, 39 U.S.C. § 117 (1990).
31. correct
32. cannot use *supra* in briefs and memoranda to cite to constitutions, statutes, or cases
33. *United States v. Claussen*, 613 F. Supp. 296 (E.D.N.Y. 1989).
34. correct
35. *Davis v. Central R.R.*, 509 F.2d 199, 201 (8th Cir. 1988).
36. d
37. *supra* = cited in full above, before; *infra* = cited in full below, following
38. True
39. False
40. False
41. False
42. False
43. c
44. c
45. a
46. b
47. True
48. True
49. False
50. True
51. stare decisis
52. res ipsa loquitor
53. jury
54. res judicata or adjudicated
55. N.B.

PRIMARY LAW IN THE FEDERAL SYSTEM

Legislative *statutory*	Constitution *statutory*	Executive *statutory*	Judicial *case law*

Statutes
• legislative bill
• slip law
• session laws - Stat. (chronological, official)
• codification - U.S.C. (by topic, official)
  - U.S.C.A. (by topic, unofficial)
  - U.S.C.S. (by topic, unofficial)
 	
Procedural Rules
• Federal Rules of Civil Procedure
  - U.S.C.A. and U.S.C.S. separate volumes
  - F.R.D. *case law*
• Federal Rules of Criminal Procedure
  - U.S.C.A. and U.S.C.S. separate volumes
  - F.R.D. *case law*
• Federal Rules of Evidence
 	
Local Court Rules
 	
Administrative Rules & Regulations
• Fed. Reg. (chronological)
• C.F.R. (by topic)
		Executive Order
		
		Presidential Proclamation
		
		Treaty
			U. S. Supreme Court
			• slip opinion
			• advance sheets
			  - U.S.L.W. (BNA)
			  - S. Ct. Bulletin (Comm. Clrng. Hse.)
			• reporter
			  - U.S. (official)
			  - S. Ct. (unofficial - West)
			  - L. Ed. 2d (unofficial - Lawyers Co-op)
			
			U. S. Court of Appeals
			• slip opinion
			• advance sheets
			• reporter
			  - F. 2d (unofficial - West)
			  - selected cases only
			
			U. S. District Court
			• slip opinion
			• advance sheets
			• reporter
			  - F. Supp. (unofficial - West)
			  - selected cases only
			  - includes Ct. of Int'l Trade cases

To find: use statutory index

To update: use statutory supplement and Shepard's Statute Citators

To find: use digest

To update: use Shepard's Case Citators

WEEK FOUR:
THE AMERICAN LEGAL SYSTEM

LESSON PLAN

- Communications Worksheet (10 minutes); go over answers; students grade own
- General Law Quiz (30 minutes); go over answers; students grade own
- Provide chart for federal courts; Constitution and Bill of Rights

GENERAL LAW, THE AMERICAN LEGAL SYSTEM—GENERAL DESCRIPTION

Working within the American legal system demands knowledge of how laws are made, the foundations of law (i.e., the U.S. Constitution), and the structure of the state and federal branches of government and the court system. These concepts provide the foundation for every legal practice area that exists. (***Note:*** *This corresponds to the section of the Certified Paralegal Examination entitled* Substantive Law—American Legal System.)

Major subject areas of this section are:

Legal terminology
Court system
Sources and classifications of law
Branches of government
Legal concepts and principles
Remedies and dispute resolution

SUGGESTED TEXT AND REFERENCES

Carper, Donald L., Mietus, Norbert J., Shoemaker, Thaddeus E., and West, Bill W., *Understanding the Law*, 6th Ed., 2010, 2008 South-Western, Cengage Learning.

Koerselman-Newman, Virginia, J. D., in cooperation with the National Association of Legal Assistants, Inc., *Certified Paralegal Review Manual: A Practical Guide to CP Exam Preparation,* 4th Ed., 2014, Delmar, Cengage Learning.

National Association of Legal Assistants, Inc., *NALA Manual for Paralegals and Legal Assistants*, 5th Ed., 2010, Delmar, Cengage Learning.

Walston-Dunham, Beth, *Introduction to Law*, 6th Ed., 2012, Delmar, Cengage Learning.

WEEK FOUR: COMMUNICATIONS WORKSHEET

Make corrections as necessary to the following sentences. Write "C" in front of those sentences that are correct as written.

1. Joyce is a person of high principals.

2. Max has been to the doctor's office many times before he found out what was wrong.

3. The person that gave me the book was quite unique.

4. A large percent of applicants enrolled in the review course.

5. Ruby is entitled to commissions, none of which were paid to her.

6. Many actors are favorably biased about liberal causes.

7. Andrew declared, "Contrary to statistical data, no one meets the criteria of the term average."

8. Did Mary seem upset when she said, "I will not work every weekend."?

9. In my opinion, due to the fact that few people pass all of the examination on the first attempt, everyone should be studying as far ahead as they can.

10. Ruth claims that Joe consented to taking her place.

11. Benjamin wondered, "Where are the supplements for the code"?

12. The defendant must testify; otherwise, his case will be much more tenable.

13. We successfully resisted the temptation to leave early.

14. The American voters must choose from among the three presidential candidates.

15. He said that he hit the plaintiff's car immediately after the accident.

Match each term in the left column with the most correct definition or synonym from the right column.

16. _____ obdurate

17. _____ ensconced

18. _____ refulgent

19. _____ elocution

20. _____ empathy

21. _____ imitable

22. _____ petulant

23. _____ vociferous

24. _____ quixotic

25. _____ compendium

a. snug, sunk into
b. clarify
c. peevish
d. worthy of being copied
e. syllabus, summary
f. noisy
g. impractical
h. glowing
i. to settle; to place or conceal in a secure place
j. future perfection in the world
k. oratory
l. identifying with and understanding another's situation
m. offensive
n. worldly, nonspiritual
o. hardened in wrong doing

Choose the most correct answer unless you are instructed to do otherwise.

26. True or False. If a court enters an order sua sponte, the court enters the order on its own motion rather than on the motion of counsel.

27. The science or system of law is called
   a. jurisprudence.
   b. jurisdiction.
   c. jus tertii.
   d. lex nexus.

28. The power of a court to hear a particular matter and to render a decision on the merits is determined by the court's
   a. jurisprudence.
   b. jurisdiction.
   c. judicature.
   d. adjudication.

For the next group of questions, fill in each blank with the term or phrase that best fits the definition shown.

29. _____ notice of suit issued by court to a defendant

30. _____ rendered by a jury at the end of a trial

31. _____ false testimony given under oath

GENERAL LAW, THE AMERICAN LEGAL SYSTEM QUIZ

Choose the most correct answer unless you are instructed to do otherwise.

1. True or False. The Bill of Rights includes the Fourteenth Amendment.

2. True or False. Congress is empowered by Article III of the Constitution to create all federal courts.

3. True or False. A bill of attainder is a law directed against a particular person or against a particular group and is forbidden specifically by Article I of the Constitution.

4. True or False. The right of privacy is contained in the Third Amendment of the Constitution.

5. True or False. The doctrine of judicial review was established in the case of *Marbury v. Madison.*

6. True or False. Arbitration is binding upon the participants, but mediation is not binding.

7. True or False. Common law has existed for as long as human beings have lived on the earth.

8. True or False. Federal diversity jurisdiction exists when no defendant is from the same state as any plaintiff and when the amount in controversy is $50,000, exclusive of interest and costs.

9. True or False. A uniform law is a law that is identical in each of the 50 states.

10. True or False. The terms *adjective law* and *procedural law* are synonymous.

11. Which of the following never can be waived by the parties or by the court?
   a. personal jurisdiction
   b. subject matter jurisdiction
   c. jury trials in criminal cases
   d. minimum contacts

12. The place where a case is tried is determined by principles of
   a. venue.
   b. jurisdiction.
   c. comity.
   d. standing.

13. Which of the following constitute mandatory law in the state courts of New York?
    a. federal law, state law, and civil law
    b. federal statutes, federal Constitution, and federal procedure law
    c. federal statutes, federal Constitution, and civil law
    d. state statutes, federal Constitution, and common law

14. Congress enacted a statute yesterday that provides that anyone convicted of a state or federal obscenity law between January and December 1993 shall be subject to an additional mandatory 5-year jail term. This statute most likely violates the Constitution as a(n)
    a. bill of attainder.
    b. ipso facto law.
    c. ex post facto law.
    d. habeas corpus law.

15. Conflict of laws statutes are designed to
    a. give the plaintiff his or her day in court.
    b. prevent forum shopping.
    c. eliminate conflicting procedural laws.
    d. prevent the plaintiff from filing multiple suits.

16. True or False. A state legislature may establish a state post office system, provided that the post office operates only intrastate.

17. True or False. Congress may reduce or enlarge the subject matter jurisdiction of the U.S. District Court.

18. True or False. Laws relating to inter vivos trusts are examples of private laws.

19. True or False. The U.S. Supreme Court is comprised of seven justices.

20. True or False. The doctrine by which powers are divided between the federal government and the states is called separation of powers.

21. The legal doctrine that prevents a person from seeking relief on the same issues and against the same parties is called
    a. res gestae.
    b. res judicata.
    c. adjudication.
    d. bar.

22. Defendants do not have to testify against themselves in a criminal trial. This is because of the prohibition contained in
    a. Article V of the Constitution.
    b. the Fourteenth Amendment.
    c. the Fourth Amendment.
    d. the Fifth Amendment.

23. Dan learns that Mary Lou plans to distribute brochures portraying him as a thief and a cheat, which are untrue statements. Dan's most viable remedy is
    a. an injunction.
    b. a suit for damages based on slander.
    c. a suit for damages based on libel.
    d. a criminal charge for misprision of a felony.

24. Copyright cases are appealed to the
    a. U.S. Court of Appeals for the circuit in which the federal trial court is located.
    b. U.S. Court of Appeals for the D.C. Circuit.
    c. U.S. Court of Appeals for the Federal Circuit.
    d. U.S. Court of Patent and Trademark Appeals.

25. Restitution may be awarded
    a. when the plaintiff cannot prove actual losses.
    b. in contract or tort cases.
    c. in law or equity cases.
    d. in substantive or procedural cases.

26. The right to a speedy trial is protected by the
    a. Fourth Amendment.
    b. Fifth Amendment.
    c. Sixth Amendment.
    d. Seventh Amendment.

27. If it chose to do so, Congress could change the jurisdiction of
    a. the U.S. Supreme Court.
    b. any federal court except the Supreme Court.
    c. any federal court.
    d. any state or federal court.

28. The requirement of a *Miranda* warning is based on the
    a. First Amendment.
    b. Fourth Amendment.
    c. Fifth Amendment.
    d. Sixth Amendment.

29. Generally speaking, a case is appealed to the U.S. Supreme Court by filing a
    a. petition for writ of certiorari.
    b. writ of habeas corpus.
    c. writ of certiorari.
    d. writ of mandamus.

30. Two sources of primary law are
    a. legal references and clerks of courts.
    b. legislation and statutory law.
    c. U.S. Supreme Court and case law.
    d. court decisions and legislative enactments.

31. True or False. States are required to ensure due process of law because of the Fifth and Fifteenth Amendments.

32. True or False. Justices of the U.S. Supreme Court are chosen by appointment of the President and approval of the House of Representatives.

33. True or False. The U.S. Supreme Court and the U.S. District Court have concurrent, original jurisdiction of matters involving foreign ambassadors.

34. True or False. If the President vetoes a bill passed by Congress, Congress may override the veto by a vote of both houses.

35. True or False. If the President neither signs nor vetoes a bill passed by Congress, the bill cannot become law.

36. True or False. Judges of the federal district court are appointed by the federal Court of Appeals, with approval of the President.

37. True or False. A person who counterfeits money may be prosecuted by either the state or federal government.

38. True or False. The U.S. Constitution requires a state to give full faith and credit to the laws of sister states.

39. True or False. Uniform laws are those statutory laws that have been adopted in substantially the same form in all 50 states.

40. True or False. An administrative agency may adopt statutes that fit within the authority established by its enabling act.

41. True or False. The federal government is one of unlimited powers.

42. Which of the following is (are) not a uniform law?
    a. UCC
    b. URESA
    c. ERISA
    d. a and b
    e. none of the above

43. Federal courts exercise
    a. limited jurisdiction only.
    b. general jurisdiction only.
    c. exclusive jurisdiction only.
    d. a and c

44. A state must have minimum contacts with a defendant to exercise jurisdiction through its long arm statute. Within this context, minimum contacts is a concept of
    a. equal protection.
    b. due process.
    c. sovereign states doctrine.
    d. privacy.
    e. none of the above

45. Conflict of law principles apply to
    a. substantive law issues in diversity cases.
    b. procedural law issues in diversity cases.
    c. substantive law issues in federal question cases.
    d. procedural law issues in federal question cases.

46. A legislative bill is an example of
    a. statutory law.
    b. case law.
    c. hypothetical law.
    d. none of the above

47. An administrative rule or regulation is an example of
    a. statutory law.
    b. case law.
    c. federal law.
    d. secondary law.

48. Rule 33 of the Federal Rules of Civil Procedure is an example of
    a. statutory law.
    b. case law.
    c. administrative law.
    d. secondary law.

49. True or False. The federal government may exercise its jurisdiction properly by setting maximum speed limits on interstate highways.

50. True or False. The Supremacy Clause of the Constitution requires sister states to enforce each other's laws when those laws are enacted properly according to due process requirements.

ANSWERS TO WEEK FOUR: COMMUNICATIONS WORKSHEET

1. wrong word—Joyce is a person of high **principles**.
2. verb tense—Max **had** been to the doctor's office many times before he found out what was wrong.
3. relative pronoun; verbose/redundant—The person **who** gave me the book was unique.
4. wrong word—A large **percentage** of applicants enrolled in the review course.
5. C
6. Many actors are biased **in favor** of liberal causes.
7. Andrew declared, "Contrary to statistical data, no one meets the criteria of the term *average*."
8. delete the period at the end of the sentence—Did Mary seem upset when she said, "I will not work every weekend"?
9. **Since** few people pass all of the examination on the first attempt, everyone should **begin** studying.
10. C
11. Benjamin wondered, "Where are the supplements for the code?"
12. wrong word—The defendant must testify; otherwise, his case will be much more **tenuous.**
13. verbose—We resisted the temptation to leave early.
14. double preposition—The American voters must choose among the three presidential candidates.
15. not clear—Did he hit the car after the accident, or did he say this after the accident?—He said that he hit the plaintiff's car immediately after the accident.
16. o
17. i
18. h
19. k
20. l
21. d
22. c
23. f
24. g
25. e
26. True
27. a
28. b
29. summons or complaint
30. verdict
31. perjury

ANSWERS TO GENERAL LAW, THE AMERICAN LEGAL SYSTEM QUIZ

1. False	14. c	27. b	40. False
2. False	15. b	28. c	41. False
3. True	16. False	29. a	42. c
4. False	17. True	30. d	43. a
5. True	18. True	31. False	44. b
6. True	19. False	32. False	45. a
7. False	20. False	33. True	46. d
8. False	21. b	34. True	47. a
9. False	22. d	35. False	48. a
10. True	23. c	36. False	49. False
11. b	24. c	37. False	50. False
12. a	25. b	38. False	
13. d	26. c	39. False	

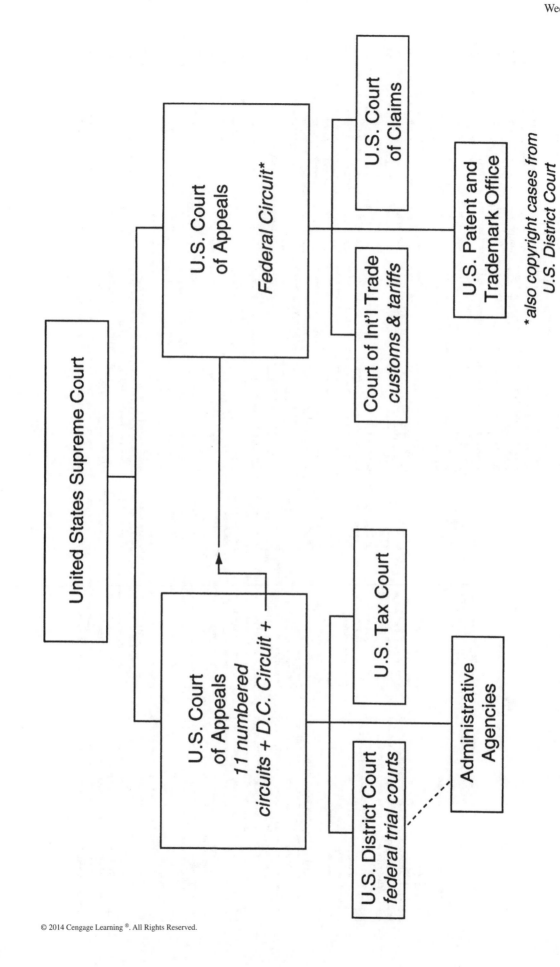

THE FEDERAL COURT SYSTEM

United States Supreme Court

U.S. Court of Appeals
Federal Circuit*

U.S. Court of Claims

Court of Int'l Trade
customs & tariffs

U.S. Patent and Trademark Office

*also copyright cases from U.S. District Court

U.S. Court of Appeals
11 numbered circuits + D.C. Circuit +

U.S. Tax Court

U.S. District Court
federal trial courts

Administrative Agencies

THE CONSTITUTION OF THE UNITED STATES OF AMERICA

We the People of the United States, in Order to form a more perfect Union, establish Justice, insure domestic Tranquility, provide for the common defence, promote the general Welfare, and secure the Blessings of Liberty to ourselves and our Posterity, do ordain and establish this CONSTITUTION for the United States of America.

ARTICLE I

Section 1. All legislative Powers herein granted shall be vested in a Congress of the United States, which shall consist of a Senate and House of Representatives.

Section 2. [1] The House of Representatives shall be composed of Members chosen every second Year by the People of the several States, and the Electors in each State shall have the Qualifications requisite for Electors of the most numerous Branch of the State Legislature.

[2] No person shall be a Representative who shall not have attained to the Age of twenty-five Years, and been seven Years a Citizen of the United States, and who shall not, when elected, be an Inhabitant of that State in which he shall be chosen.

[3] Representatives and direct Taxes shall be apportioned among the several States which may be included within this Union, according to their respective Numbers, which shall be determined by adding to the whole Number of free Persons, including those bound to Service for a Term of Years, and excluding Indians not taxed, three fifths of all other Persons. The actual Enumeration shall be made within three Years after the first Meeting of the Congress of the United States, and within every subsequent Term of ten Years, in such Manner as they shall by Law direct. The Number of Representatives shall not exceed one for every thirty Thousand, but each State shall have at Least one Representative; and until such enumeration shall be made, the State of New Hampshire shall be entitled to chuse three, Massachusetts eight, Rhode-Island and Providence Plantations one, Connecticut five, New York six, New Jersey four, Pennsylvania eight, Delaware one, Maryland six, Vir-

ginia ten, North Carolina five, South Carolina five, and Georgia three.

[4] When vacancies happen in the Representation from any State, the Executive Authority thereof shall issue Writs of Election to fill such Vacancies.

[5] The House of Representatives shall chuse their Speaker and other Officers; and shall have the sole Power of Impeachment.

Section 3. [1] The Senate of the United States shall be composed of two Senators from each State, chosen by the Legislature thereof, for six Years; and each Senator shall have one Vote.

[2] Immediately after they shall be assembled in Consequence of the first Election, they shall be divided as equally as may be into three Classes. The Seats of the Senators of the first Class shall be vacated at the Expiration of the Second Year, of the second Class at the Expiration of the fourth Year, and of the third Class at the Expiration of the sixth Year, so that one-third may be chosen every second Year; and if Vacancies happen by Resignation, or otherwise, during the Recess of the Legislature of any State, the Executive thereof may make temporary Appointments until the next Meeting of the Legislature, which shall then fill such Vacancies.

[3] No person shall be a Senator who shall not have attained to the Age of thirty Years, and been nine Years a Citizen of the United States, and who shall not, when elected, be an Inhabitant of that State for which he shall be chosen.

[4] The Vice President of the United States shall be President of the Senate, but shall have no Vote, unless they be equally divided.

[5] The Senate shall chuse their Officers, and also a President pro tempore, in the absence of the Vice President, or when he shall exercise the Office of President of the United States.

[6] The Senate shall have the sole Power to try all Impeachments. When sitting for that Purpose, they shall be on Oath or Affirmation. When the President of the United States is tried, the Chief Justice shall preside. And no Person shall be convicted without the Concurrence of two-thirds of the Members present.

[7] Judgment in Cases of Impeachment shall not extend further than to removal from Office, and disqualification to hold and enjoy any Office of honor, Trust, or Profit under the United States: but the Party convicted shall nevertheless be liable and subject to Indictment, Trial, Judgment, and Punishment, according to Law.

Section 4. [1] The Times, Places and Manner of holding Elections for Senators and Representatives, shall be prescribed in each State by the Legislature thereof; but the Congress may at any time by Law make or alter such Regulations, except as to the Places of chusing Senators.

[2] The Congress shall assemble at least once in every Year, and such Meeting shall be on the first Monday in December, unless they shall by Law appoint a different Day.

Section 5. [1] Each House shall be the Judge of the Elections, Returns, and Qualifications of its own Members, and a Majority of each shall constitute a Quorum to do Business; but a smaller Number may adjourn from day to day, and may be authorized to compel the Attendance of absent Members, in such Manner, and under such Penalties as each House may provide.

[2] Each House may determine the Rules of its Proceedings, punish its Members for disorderly Behavior, and with the Concurrence of two thirds, expel a Member.

[3] Each House shall keep a Journal of its Proceedings, and from time to time publish the same, excepting such Parts as may in their Judgment require Secrecy; and the Yeas and Nays of the Members of either House on any question shall, at the Desire of one fifth of those Present, be entered on the Journal.

[4] Neither House, during the Session of Congress, shall, without the Consent of the other, adjourn for more than three days, nor to any other Place than that in which the Two Houses shall be sitting.

Section 6. [1] The Senators and Representatives shall receive a Compensation for their Services, to be ascertained by Law, and paid out of the Treasury of the United States. They shall in all Cases, except Treason, Felony and Breach of the Peace, be privileged from Arrest during their Attendance at the Session of their respective Houses, and in going to and return-

ing from the same; and for any Speech or Debate in either House, they shall not be questioned in any other Place.

[2] No Senator or Representative shall, during the Time for which he was elected, be appointed to any civil Office under the Authority of the United States, which shall have been created, or the Emoluments whereof shall have been encreased during such time; and no Person holding any Office under the United States, shall be a Member of either House during his Continuance in Office.

Section 7. [1] All Bills for raising Revenue shall originate in the House of Representatives; but the Senate may propose or concur with Amendments as on other Bills.

[2] Every Bill shall have passed the House of Representatives and the Senate, shall, before it become a Law, be presented to the President of the United States; if he approve he shall sign it, but if not he shall return it, with his Objections to that House in which it shall have originated, who shall enter the Objections at large on their Journal, and proceed to reconsider it. If after such Reconsideration two thirds of that House shall agree to pass the Bill, it shall be sent, together with the Objections, to the other House, by which it shall likewise be reconsidered, and if approved by two thirds of that House, it shall become a Law. But in all such Cases, the Votes of both Houses shall be determined by Yeas and Nays, and the Names of the Persons voting for and against the Bill shall be entered on the Journal of each House respectively. If any Bill shall not be returned by the President within ten Days (Sundays excepted) after it shall have been presented to him, the Same shall be a Law, in like Manner as if he had signed it, unless the Congress by their Adjournment prevent its Return, in which Case it shall not be a Law.

[3] Every Order, Resolution, or Vote to which the Concurrence of the Senate and House of Representatives may be necessary (except on a question of Adjournment) shall be presented to the President of the United States; and before the Same shall take Effect, shall be approved by him, or being disapproved by him shall be repassed by two thirds of the Senate and House of Representatives, according to the Rules and Limitations prescribed in the Case of a Bill.

Section 8. The Congress shall have Power

[1] To lay and collect Taxes, Duties, Imposts and Excises, to pay the Debts and provide for the common Defence and general Welfare of the United States; but all Duties, Imposts and Excises shall be uniform throughout the United States;

[2] To borrow money on the credit of the United States;

[3] To regulate Commerce with foreign Nations, and among the several States, and with the Indian Tribes;

[4] To establish an uniform Rule of Naturalization, and uniform Laws on the subject of Bankruptcies throughout the United States;

[5] To coin Money, regulate the Value thereof, and of foreign Coin, and fix the Standard of Weights and Measures;

[6] To provide for the Punishment of counterfeiting the Securities and current Coin of the United States;

[7] To Establish Post Offices and post Roads;

[8] To promote the Progress of Science and useful Arts, by securing for limited Times to Authors and Inventors the exclusive Right to their respective Writings and Discoveries;

[9] To constitute Tribunals inferior to the Supreme Court;

[10] To define and punish Piracies and Felonies committed on the high Seas, and Offenses against the Law of Nations;

[11] To declare War, grant Letters of Marque and Reprisal, and make Rules concerning Captures on Land and Water;

[12] To raise and support Armies, but no Appropriation of Money to that Use shall be for a longer Term than two Years;

[13] To provide and maintain a Navy;

[14] To make Rules for the Government and Regulation of the land and naval Forces;

[15] To provide for calling forth the Militia to execute the Laws of the Union, suppress Insurrections and repel Invasions;

[16] To provide for organizing, arming, and disciplining, the Militia, and for governing such Part of them as may be employed in the Service of the United States, reserving to the States respectively, the Appointment of the Officers, and the Authority of training the Militia according to the discipline prescribed by Congress;

[17] To exercise exclusive Legislation in all Cases whatsoever, over such District (not exceeding ten Miles square) as may, by Cession of particular States, and the acceptance of Congress, become the Seat of the Government of the United States, and to exercise like Authority over all Places purchased by the Consent of the Legislature of the State in which the Same shall be, for the Erection of Forts, Magazines, Arsenals, dock-Yards, and other needful Buildings;—And

[18] To make all Laws which shall be necessary and proper for carrying into Execution the foregoing Powers, and all other Powers vested by this Constitution in the Government of the United States, or in any Department or Officer thereof.

Section 9. [1] The Migration or Importation of Such Persons as any of the States now existing shall think proper to admit, shall not be prohibited by the Congress prior to the Year one thousand eight hundred and eight, but a tax or duty may be imposed on such Importation, not exceeding ten dollars for each Person.

[2] The privilege of the Writ of Habeas Corpus shall not be suspended, unless when in Cases of Rebellion or Invasion the public Safety may require it.

[3] No Bill of Attainder or ex post facto Law shall be passed.

[4] No capitation, or other direct, Tax shall be laid, unless in Proportion to the Census or Enumeration herein before directed to be taken.

[5] No Tax or Duty shall be laid on Articles exported from any State.

[6] No preference shall be given by any Regulation of Commerce or Revenue to the Ports of one State over those of another; nor shall Vessels bound to, or from, one State be obliged to enter, clear, or pay Duties in another.

[7] No money shall be drawn from the Treasury, but in Consequence of Appropriations made by Law; and a regular Statement and Account of the Receipts and Expenditures of all public Money shall be published from time to time.

[8] No Title of Nobility shall be granted by the United States: And no Person holding any Office of Profit or Trust under them, shall, without the Consent of the Congress, accept of any present, Emolument, Office, or Title, of any kind whatever, from any King, Prince, or foreign State.

Section 10. [1] No State shall enter into any Treaty, Alliance, or Confederation; grant Letters of Marque and Reprisal; coin Money; emit Bills of Credit; make any Thing but gold and silver Coin a Tender in Payment of Debts; pass any bill of Attainder, ex post factor Law, or Law impairing the Obligation of Contracts, or grant any Title of Nobility.

[2] No State shall, without the Consent of the Congress, lay any Imposts or Duties on Imports or Exports, except what may be absolutely necessary for executing its inspection Laws: and the net Produce of all Duties and Imposts, laid by any State on Imports or Exports, shall be for the Use of the Treasury of the United States; and all such Laws shall be subject to the Revision and Control of the Congress.

[3] No State shall, without the Consent of Congress, lay any duty of Tonnage, keep Troops, or Ships of War in time of Peace, enter into any Agreement or Compact with another State, or with a foreign Power, or engage in War, unless actually invaded, or in such imminent Danger as will not admit of delay.

ARTICLE II

Section 1. [1] The executive Power shall be vested in a President of the United States of America. He shall hold his Office during the Term of four Years, and together with the Vice President, chosen for the same Term, be elected, as follows:

[2] Each State shall appoint, in such Manner as the Legislature thereof may direct, a Number of Electors, equal to the whole Number of Senators and Representatives to which the State may be entitled in the Congress: but no Senator or Representative, or Person holding an Office of Trust or Profit under the United States, shall be appointed an Elector.

[3] The Electors shall meet in their respective States, and vote by Ballot for two persons, of whom one at least shall not be an Inhabitant of the same State with themselves. And they shall make a List of all the Persons voted for, and of the Number of Votes for each; which List they shall sign and certify, and transmit sealed to the Seat of the Government of the United States, directed to the President of the Senate. The President of the Senate shall, in the Presence of the Senate and House of Representatives, open all the Certificates, and the Votes shall then be counted. The Person having the greatest Number of Votes shall be the President, if such Number be a Majority of the whole Number of Electors appointed; and if there be more than one who have such Majority, and have an equal Number of Votes, then the House of Representatives shall immediately chuse by Ballot one of them for President; and if no Person have a Majority, then from the five highest on the List the said House shall in like Manner chuse the President. But in chusing the President, the Votes shall be taken by States, the Representation from each State having one Vote; A quorum for this Purpose shall consist of a Member or Members from two-thirds of the States, and a Majority of all the States shall be necessary to a Choice. In every Case, after the Choice of the President, the Person having the greatest Number of Votes of the Electors shall be the Vice President. But if there should remain two or more who have equal Votes, the Senate shall chuse from them by Ballot the Vice President.

[4] The Congress may determine the Time of chusing the Electors, and the Day on which they shall give their Votes; which Day shall be the same throughout the United States.

[5] No person except a natural born Citizen, or a Citizen of the United States, at the time of the Adoption of this Constitution, shall be eligible to the Office of President; neither shall any Person be eligible to that Office who shall not have attained to the Age of thirty-five Years, and been fourteen Years a Resident within the United States.

[6] In case of the removal of the President from Office, or of his Death, Resignation, or Inability to discharge the Powers and Duties of the said Office, the same shall devolve on the Vice President, and the Congress may by Law provide for the Case of Removal, Death, Resignation or Inability, both of the President and Vice President, declaring what Officer shall then act as President, and such Officer shall act accordingly, until the Disability be removed, or a President shall be elected.

[7] The President shall, at stated Times, receive for his Services, a Compensation, which shall neither be encreased nor diminished during the Period for which he shall have been elected, and he shall not receive within that Period any other Emolument from the United States, or any of them.

[8] Before he enter on the Execution of his Office, he shall take the following Oath or Affirmation:—"I do solemnly swear (or affirm) that I will faithfully execute the Office of President of the United States, and will to the best of my Ability, preserve, protect and defend the Constitution of the United States."

Section 2. [1] The President shall be Commander in Chief of the Army and Navy of the United States, and of the Militia of the several States, when called into the actual Service of the United States; he may require the Opinion, in writing, of the principal Officer in each of the executive Departments, upon any subject relating to the Duties of their respective Offices, and he shall have Power to grant Reprieves and Pardons for Offenses against the United States, except in Cases of Impeachment.

[2] He shall have Power, by and with the Advice and Consent of the Senate, to make Treaties, provided two-thirds of the Senators present concur; and he shall nominate, and by and with the Advice and Consent of the Senate, shall appoint Ambassadors, other public Ministers and Consuls, Judges of the Supreme Court, and all other Officers of the United States, whose Appointments are not herein otherwise provided for, and shall be established by Law; but the Congress may by Law vest the Appointment of such inferior Officers, as they think proper, in the President alone, in the Courts of Law, or in the Heads of Departments.

[3] The President shall have Power to fill up all Vacancies that may happen during the Recess of the Senate, by granting Commissions which shall expire at the End of their next Session.

Section 3. He shall from time to time give to the Congress Information of the State of the Union, and recommend to their Consideration such Measures as he shall judge necessary and expedient; he may, on extraordinary Occasions, convene both Houses, or either of them, and in Case of Disagreement between them, with Respect to the Time of Adjournment, he may adjourn them to such Time as he shall think proper; he shall receive Ambassadors and other public Ministers; he shall take Care that the Laws be faithfully executed, and shall Commission all the Officers of the United States.

Section 4. The President, Vice President and all civil Officers of the United States, shall be removed from Office on Impeachment for, and Conviction of, Treason, Bribery, or other high Crimes and Misdemeanors.

ARTICLE III

Section 1. The judicial Power of the United States, shall be vested in one supreme Court, and in such inferior Courts as the Congress may from time to time ordain and establish. The Judges, both of the supreme and inferior Courts, shall hold their Offices during good behaviour, and shall, at stated Times, receive for their Services a Compensation which shall not be diminished during their Continuance in Office.

Section 2. [1] The judicial Power shall extend to all Cases, in Law and Equity, arising under this Constitution, the Laws of the United States, and Treaties made, or which shall be made under their Authority;—to all Cases affecting Ambassadors, other public Ministers and Consuls;—to all Cases of admiralty and maritime Jurisdiction;—to Controversies to which the United States shall be a Party;—to Controversies between two or more States;—between a State and Citizens of different States,—between Citizens of the same State claiming Lands under Grants of different States, and between a State, or the Citizens thereof, and foreign States, Citizens or Subjects.

[2] In all Cases affecting Ambassadors, other public Ministers and Consuls, and those in which a State shall be Party, the supreme Court shall have original Jurisdiction. In all the other Cases before mentioned, the supreme Court shall have appellate Jurisdiction, both as to Law and Fact, with such Exceptions, and under such Regulations as the Congress shall make.

[3] The trial of all Crimes, except in Cases of Impeachment, shall be by Jury; and such Trial shall be held in the State where the said Crimes shall have been committed; but when not committed within any State, the Trial shall be at such Place or Places as the Congress may by Law have directed.

Section 3. [1] Treason against the United States, shall consist only in levying War against them, or, in adhering to their Enemies, giving them Aid and Comfort. No Person shall be convicted of Treason unless on the Testimony of two Witnesses to the same overt Act, or on Confession in open Court.

[2] The Congress shall have power to declare the Punishment of Treason, but no Attainder of Treason shall work Corruption of Blood, or Forfeiture except during the Life of the Person attainted.

ARTICLE IV

Section 1. Full Faith and Credit shall be given in each State to the public Acts, Records, and judicial Proceedings of every other State. And the Congress may by general Laws prescribe the Manner in which such Acts, Records and Proceedings shall be proved, and the Effect thereof.

Section 2. [1] The Citizens of each State shall be entitled to all Privileges and Immunities of Citizens in the several States.

[2] A Person charged in any State with Treason, Felony, or other Crime, who shall flee from Justice, and be found in another State, shall on demand of the executive Authority of the State from which he fled, be delivered up, to be removed to the State having Jurisdiction of the Crime.

[3] No Person held to Service or Labour in one State, under the Laws thereof, escaping into another, shall, in Consequence of any Law or Regulation therein, be discharged from such Service or Labour, but shall be delivered up on Claim of the Party to whom such Service or Labour may be due.

Section 3. [1] New States may be admitted by the Congress into this Union; but no new State shall be formed or erected within the Jurisdiction of any other State; nor any State be formed by the Junction of two or more States, or parts of States, without the Consent of the Legislatures of the States concerned as well as of the Congress.

[2] The Congress shall have Power to dispose of and make all needful Rules and Regulations respecting the Territory or other Property belonging to the United States; and nothing in this Constitution shall be so construed as to Prejudice any Claims of the United States, or of any particular State.

Section 4. The United States shall guarantee to every State in this Union a Republican Form of Government, and shall protect each of them against Invasion; and on Application of the Legislature, or of the Executive (when the Legislature cannot be convened) against domestic Violence.

ARTICLE V

The Congress, whenever two-thirds of both Houses shall deem it necessary, shall propose Amendments to this Constitution, or, on the Application of the Legislatures of two-thirds of the several States, shall call a Convention for proposing Amendments, which, in either Case, shall be valid to all Intents and Purposes, as part of this Constitution, when ratified by the Legislatures of three-fourths of the several States, or by Conventions in three-fourths thereof, as the one or the other Mode of Ratification may be proposed by the Congress; Provided that no Amendment which may be made prior to the Year One thousand eight hundred and eight shall in any Manner affect the first and fourth Clauses in the Ninth Section of the first Article; and that no State, without its Consent, shall be deprived of its equal Suffrage in the Senate.

ARTICLE VI

[1] All Debts contracted and Engagements entered into, before the Adoption of this Constitution shall be valid against the United States under this Constitution, as under the Confederation.

[2] This Constitution, and the Laws of the United States which shall be made in Pursuance thereof; and all Treaties made, or which shall be made, under the Authority of the United States, shall be the supreme Law of the Land; and the Judges in every State shall be bound thereby, any Thing in the Constitution or Laws of any State to the Contrary notwithstanding.

[3] The Senators and Representatives before mentioned, and the Members of the several State Legislatures, and all executive and judicial Officers, both of the United States and of the several States, shall be bound by Oath or Affirmation, to support this Constitution; but no religious Test shall ever be required as a Qualification to any Office or public Trust under the United States.

ARTICLE VII

The Ratification of the Conventions of nine States shall be sufficient for the Establishment of this Constitution between the States so ratifying the Same.

ARTICLES IN ADDITION TO, AND AMENDMENT OF, THE CONSTITUTION OF THE UNITED STATES OF AMERICA, PROPOSED BY CONGRESS, AND RATIFIED BY THE LEGISLATURES OF THE SEVERAL STATES, PURSUANT TO THE FIFTH ARTICLE OF THE ORIGINAL CONSTITUTION

AMENDMENT I [1791]

Congress shall make no law respecting an establishment of religion, or prohibiting the free exercise thereof; or abridging the freedom of speech, or of the press; or the right of the people peaceably to assemble and to petition the Government for a redress of grievances.

AMENDMENT II [1791]

A well regulated Militia, being necessary to the security of a free State, the right of the people to keep and bear Arms, shall not be infringed.

AMENDMENT III [1791]

No Soldier shall, in time of peace be quartered in any house, without the consent of the Owner, nor in time of war, but in a manner to be prescribed by Law.

AMENDMENT IV [1791]

The right of the people to be secure in their persons, houses, papers, and effects, against unreasonable searches and seizures, shall not be violated, and no Warrants shall issue, but upon probable cause, supported by Oath or affirmation, and particularly describing the place to be searched, and the persons or things to be seized.

AMENDMENT V [1791]

No person shall be held to answer for a capital, or otherwise infamous crime, unless on a presentment or indictment of a Grand Jury, except in cases arising in the land or naval forces, or in the Militia, when in actual service in time of War or public danger; nor shall any person be subject for the same offence to be twice put in jeopardy of life or limb; nor shall he be compelled in any criminal case to be a witness against himself, nor be deprived of life, liberty, or property, without due process of law; nor shall private property be taken for public use, without just compensation.

AMENDMENT VI [1791]

In all criminal prosecutions, the accused shall enjoy the right to a speedy and public trial, by an impartial jury of the State and district wherein the crime shall have been committed, which district shall have been previously ascertained by law, and to be informed of the nature and cause of the accusation; to be confronted with the witnesses against him; to have compulsory process for obtaining witnesses in his favor, and to have the Assistance of Counsel for his defence.

AMENDMENT VII [1791]

In suits at common law, where the value in controversy shall exceed twenty dollars, the right of trial by jury shall be preserved, and no fact tried by a jury, shall be otherwise reexamined in any Court of the United States, than according to the rules of the common law.

AMENDMENT VIII [1791]

Excessive bail shall not be required, nor excessive fines imposed, nor cruel and unusual punishments inflicted.

AMENDMENT IX [1791]

The enumeration in the Constitution, of certain rights, shall not be construed to deny or disparage others retained by the people.

AMENDMENT X [1791]

The powers not delegated to the United States by the Constitution, nor prohibited by it to the States, are reserved to the States respectively, or to the people.

AMENDMENT XI [1798]

The Judicial power of the United States shall not be construed to extend to any suit in law or equity, commenced or prosecuted against one of the United States by Citizens of another State, or by Citizens or Subjects of any Foreign State.

AMENDMENT XII [1804]

The electors shall meet in their respective states and vote by ballot for President and Vice-President, one of whom, at least, shall not be an inhabitant of the same state with themselves; they shall name in their ballots the person voted for as President, and in distinct ballots the person voted for as Vice-President, and they shall make distinct lists of all persons voted for as President, and of all persons voted for as Vice-President, and of the number of votes for each, which lists they shall sign and certify, and transmit sealed to the seat of the government of the United States, directed to the President of the Senate;—The President of the Senate shall, in presence of the Senate and House of Representatives, open all the certificates and the votes shall then be counted;—The person having the greatest number of votes for President, shall be the President, if such number be a majority of the whole number of Electors appointed; and if no person have such majority, then from the persons having the highest numbers not exceeding three on the list of those voted for as President, the House of Representatives shall choose immediately, by ballot, the President. But in choosing the President, the votes shall be taken by states, the representation from each state having one vote; a quorum for this purpose shall consist of a member or members from two-thirds of the states, and a majority of all the states shall be necessary to a choice. And if the House of Representatives shall not choose a President whenever the right of choice shall devolve upon them, before the fourth day of March next following, then the Vice-President shall act as President, as in the case of the death or other constitutional disability of the President. — The person having the greatest number of votes as Vice-President, shall be the Vice-President, if such number be a majority of the whole number of Electors appointed, and if no person have a majority, then from the two highest numbers on the list, the Senate shall choose the Vice-President; a quorum for the purpose shall consist of two-thirds of the whole number of Senators, and a majority of the whole number shall be necessary to a choice. But no person constitutionally ineligible to the office of President shall be eligible to that of Vice-President of the United States.

AMENDMENT XIII [1865]

Section 1. Neither slavery nor involuntary servitude, except as a punishment for crime whereof the party shall have been duly convicted, shall exist within the United States, or any place subject to their jurisdiction.

Section 2. Congress shall have power to enforce this article by appropriate legislation.

AMENDMENT XIV [1868]

Section 1. All persons born or naturalized in the United States, and subject to the jurisdiction thereof, are citizens of the United States and of the State wherein they reside. No State shall make or enforce any law which shall abridge the privileges or immunities of citizens of the United States; nor shall any State deprive any person of life, liberty, or property, without due process of law; nor deny to any person within its jurisdiction the equal protection of the laws.

Section 2. Representatives shall be apportioned among the several States according to their respective numbers, counting the whole number of persons in each State, excluding Indians not taxed. But when the right to vote at any election for the choice of electors for President and Vice-President of the United States, Representatives in Congress, the Executive and Judicial officers of a State, or the members of the Legislature thereof, is denied to any of the male inhabitants of such State, being twenty-one years of age, and citizens of the United States, or in any way abridged, except for participation in rebellion, or other crime, the basis of representation therein shall be reduced in the proportion which the number of such male citizens shall bear to the whole number of male citizens twenty-one years of age in such State.

Section 3. No person shall be a Senator or Representative in Congress, or elector of President and Vice-President, or hold any office, civil or military, under the United States, or under any State, who, having previously taken an oath, as a member of Congress, or as an officer of the United States, or as an executive or judicial officer of any State, to support the Constitution of the United States, shall have engaged in insurrection or rebellion against the same, or given aid or comfort to the enemies thereof. But Congress may by a vote of two-thirds of each House, remove such disability.

Section 4. The validity of the public debt of the United States, authorized by law, including debts incurred for payment of pensions and bounties for services in suppressing insurrection or rebellion, shall not be questioned. But neither the United States nor any State shall assume or pay any debt or obligation incurred in aid of insurrection or rebellion against the United States, or any claim for the loss or emancipation of any slave; but all such debts, obligations and claims shall be held illegal and void.

Section 5. The Congress shall have power to enforce, by appropriate legislation, the provisions of this article.

AMENDMENT XV [1870]

Section 1. The right of citizens of the United States to vote shall not be denied or abridged by the United States or by any State on account of race, color, or previous condition of servitude.

Section 2. The Congress shall have power to enforce this article by appropriate legislation.

AMENDMENT XVI [1913]

The Congress shall have power to lay and collect taxes on incomes, from whatever source derived, without apportionment among the several States, and without regard to any census or enumeration.

AMENDMENT XVII [1913]

The Senate of the United States shall be composed of two Senators from each State, elected by the people thereof, for six years; and each Senator shall have one vote. The electors in each State shall have the qualifications requisite for electors of the most numerous branch of the State legislatures.

When vacancies happen in the representation of any State in the Senate, the executive authority of such State shall issue writs of election to fill such vacancies: *Provided,* That the legislature of any State may empower the executive thereof to make temporary appointments until the people fill the vacancies by election as the legislature may direct.

This amendment shall not be so construed as to affect the election or term of any Senator chosen before it becomes valid as part of the Constitution.

AMENDMENT XVIII [1919]

Section 1. After one year from the ratification of this article the manufacture, sale, or transportation of intoxicating liquors within, the importation thereof into, or the exportation thereof from the United States and all territory subject to the jurisdiction thereof for beverage purposes is hereby prohibited.

Section 2. The Congress and the several States shall have concurrent power to enforce this article by appropriate legislation.

Section 3. This article shall be inoperative unless it shall have been ratified as an amendment to the Constitution by the legislatures of the several States, as provided in the Constitution, within seven years from the date of submission hereof to the States by the Congress.

AMENDMENT XIX [1920]

The right of citizens of the United States to vote shall not be denied or abridged by the United States or by any State on account of sex.

Congress shall have the power to enforce this article by appropriate legislation.

AMENDMENT XX [1933]

Section 1. The terms of the President and Vice President shall end at noon on the 20th day of January, and the terms of Senators and Representatives at noon on the 3d day of January, of the years in which such terms would have ended if this article had not been ratified; and the terms of their successors shall then begin.

Section 2. The Congress shall assemble at least once in every year, and such meeting shall begin at noon on the 3d day of January, unless they shall by law appoint a different day.

Section 3. If, at the time fixed for the beginning of the term of the President, the President elect shall have died, the Vice President elect shall become President. If a President shall not have been chosen before the time fixed for the beginning of his term, or if the President elect shall have failed to qualify, then the Vice President elect shall act as President until a President shall have qualified; and the Congress may by law provide for the case wherein neither a President elect nor a Vice President elect shall have qualified, declaring who shall then act as President, or the manner in which one who is to act shall be selected, and such person shall act accordingly until a President or Vice President shall have qualified.

Section 4. The Congress may by law provide for the case of the death of any of the persons from whom the House of Representative may choose a President whenever the right of choice shall have devolved upon them, and for the case of the death of any of the persons from whom the Senate may choose a Vice President whenever the right of choice shall have devolved upon them.

Section 5. Sections 1 and 2 shall take effect on the 15th day of October following the ratification of this article.

Section 6. This article shall be inoperative unless it shall have been ratified as an amendment to the Constitution by the legislatures of three-fourths of the several States within seven years from the date of its submission.

AMENDMENT XXI [1933]

Section 1. The eighteenth article of amendment to the Constitution of the United States is hereby repealed.

Section 2. The transportation or importation into any State, Territory, or possession of the United States for delivery or use therein of intoxicating liquors, in violation of the laws thereof, is hereby prohibited.

Section 3. This article shall be inoperative unless it shall have been ratified as an amendment to the Constitution by conventions in the several States, as provided in the Constitution, within seven years from the date of the submission hereof to the States by the Congress.

AMENDMENT XXII [1951]

Section 1. No person shall be elected to the office of the President more than twice, and no person who has held the office of President, or acted as President, for more than two years of a term to which some other person was elected President shall be elected to the office of the President more than once. But this Article shall not apply to any person holding the office of President when this Article was proposed by the Congress, and shall not prevent any person who may be holding the office of President, or acting as President, during the term within which the Article becomes operative from holding the office of President or acting as President during the remainder of such term.

Section 2. This article shall be inoperative unless it shall have been ratified as an amendment to the Constitution by the legislatures of three-fourths of the several States within seven years from the date of its submission to the States by Congress.

AMENDMENT XXIII [1961]

Section 1. The District constituting the seat of Government of the United States shall appoint in such manner as the Congress may direct:

A number of electors of President and Vice President equal to the whole number of Senators and Representatives in Congress to which the District would be entitled if it were a State, but in no event more than the least populous State; they shall be in addition to those appointed by the States, but they shall be considered, for the purposes of the election of President and Vice President, to be electors appointed by a State; and they shall meet in the District and perform such duties as provided by the twelfth article of amendment.

Section 2. The Congress shall have power to enforce this article by appropriate legislation.

AMENDMENT XXIV [1964]

Section 1. The right of citizens of the United States to vote in any primary or other election for President or Vice President, for electors for President or Vice President, or for Senator or Representative in Congress, shall not be denied or abridged by the United States or any State by reason of failure to pay any poll tax or other tax.

Section 2. The Congress shall have power to enforce this article by appropriate legislation.

AMENDMENT XXV [1967]

Section 1. In case of the removal of the President from office or his death or resignation, the Vice President shall become President.

Section 2. Whenever there is a vacancy in the office of the Vice President, the President shall nominate a Vice President who shall take the Office upon confirmation by a majority vote of both houses of Congress.

Section 3. Whenever the President transmits to the President pro tempore of the Senate and the Speaker of the House of Representatives his written declaration that he is unable to discharge the powers and duties of his office, and until he transmits to them a written declaration to the contrary, such powers and duties shall be discharged by the Vice President as Acting President.

Section 4. Whenever the Vice President and a majority of either the principal officers of the executive departments, or of such other body as Congress may by law provide, transmit to the President pro tempore of the Senate and the Speaker of the House of Representatives their written declaration that the President is unable to discharge the powers and duties of his office, the Vice President shall immediately assume the powers and duties of the office as Acting President.

Thereafter, when the President transmits to the President pro tempore of the Senate and the Speaker of the House of Representatives his written declaration that no inability exists, he shall resume the powers and duties of his office unless the Vice President and a majority of either the principal officers of the executive department, or of such other body as Congress may by law provide, transmit within four days to the President pro tempore of the Senate and the Speaker of the House of Representatives their written declaration that the President is unable to discharge the powers and duties of his office. Thereupon Congress shall decide the issue, assembling within 48 hours for that purpose if not in session. If the Congress, within 21 days after receipt of the latter written declaration, or, if Congress is not in session, within 21 days after Congress is required to assemble, determines by two-thirds vote of both houses that the President is unable to discharge the powers and duties of his office, the Vice President shall continue to discharge the same as Acting President; otherwise, the President shall resume the powers and duties of his office.

AMENDMENT XXVI [1971]

Section 1. The right of citizens of the United States, who are eighteen years of age, or older, to vote shall not be denied or abridged by the United States or by any state on account of age.

Section 2. The Congress shall have the power to enforce this article by appropriate legislation.

AMENDMENT XXVII [1992]

No law, varying the compensation for the services of the Senators and Representatives, shall take effect, until an election of Representatives shall have intervened.

WEEK FIVE: ETHICS

LESSON PLAN

- Communications Worksheet (10 minutes); go over answers; students grade own
- Ethics Quiz (30 minutes); go over answers

ETHICS—GENERAL DESCRIPTION

Paralegals occupy positions of trust in their communications and have daily contact with clients, employers, coworkers, and the general public. Paralegals must maintain high levels of competency and must refrain from the unauthorized practice of law. This section of the Certified Paralegal Examination is composed of questions covering areas listed in this chapter. In addition, questions related to ethics and professional responsibility are included in all sections of the examination.

Major subject areas of this section are:

Ethical responsibilities centering on performance of delegated work
Paralegal professional responsibility
Professional relationships
Client and public contact
Attorney code of ethics and discipline

SUGGESTED TEXT AND REFERENCES

American Bar Association, *Model Rules of Professional Conduct*, latest edition.

Cannon, Therese A., J. D., *Ethics and Professional Responsibility for Legal Assistants*, 2011, 6th Ed., Aspen College Series, Wolters Kluwer Law & Business.

Elkins, Thomas L., and Shaffer, James R., *Legal Interviewing and Counseling in a Nutshell*, 4th Ed., 2004, Thomson Reuters Westlaw.

Koerselman-Newman, Virginia, J. D., in cooperation with the National Association of Legal Assistants, Inc., *Certified Paralegal Review Manual: A Practical Guide to CP Exam Preparation*, 4th Ed., 2014, Delmar, Cengage Learning.

NALA Code of Ethics and Professional Responsibility, Tulsa, Oklahoma, http://www.nala.org

NALA Model Standards and Guidelines for Utilization of Paralegals, Tulsa, Oklahoma, http://www.nala.org

National Association of Legal Assistants, Inc., *NALA Manual for Paralegals and Legal Assistants*, 5th Ed., 2010, Delmar, Cengage Learning.

WEEK FIVE: COMMUNICATIONS WORKSHEET

Make corrections as necessary to the following sentences. Write "C" in front of those sentences that are correct as written.

1. The plaintiff maintains that the defendant admitted to hitting plaintiff's car.

2. Since one who takes life too seriously often may be unhappy; you should maintain a good sense of humor.

3. I am adverse to this course of action.

4. The committee selected among four well considered plans.

5. Either the judge or the members of the jury were wrong.

6. William asked, "Where are we going"?

7. Had you arrived when Amy told the audience, "This is the first day of the rest of your life"?

8. An unabridged dictionary is very useful, but they are too heavy to take to school.

9. The lucky ones are us.

10. Do you think it could have been him?

11. Whom did you say was coming?

12. It is presently Saturday, October 31.

13. Please hand me the little brown book.

14. We only had final exams last week.

15. The article, "Watch Your Money", was written by Andrew Rush, Jr.

For the next group of questions, match each term in the left column with the word, phrase, or synonym in the right column that most accurately defines or describes it.

16. _____ compunction
17. _____ cryptic
18. _____ comport
19. _____ egregious
20. _____ commodious
21. _____ malfeasance
22. _____ morass
23. _____ corpus delecti
24. _____ raze
25. _____ appellation

a. performance of unlawful act/evil wrongdoing
b. designation; name
c. spacious, roomy
d. misleading, incorrect
e. monumentally bad
f. demolish to ground level
g. hidden
h. carry in a particular manner; carry oneself
i. guilty uneasiness
j. infirm
k. quagmire
l. hidden
m. transparent
n. essence of the crime

ETHICS QUIZ

Choose the most correct answer unless you are instructed to do otherwise.

1. The objective(s) of professional ethics for paralegals is to
   a. take advantage of educational opportunities.
   b. maintain a high level of competency.
   c. refrain from the unauthorized practice of law.
   d. a and c
   e. all of the above

2. Any paralegal who violates a UPL statute may incur one or more of the following sanctions:
   a. criminal prosecution
   b. civil liability to any alien damaged by the negligence of the paralegal while engaging in unauthorized acts
   c. termination of employment
   d. all of the above
   e. none of the above

3. True or False. A written set of rules governing professional conduct is known as a code.

4. True or False. The practice of law is any act that involves giving legal advice or opinions to others or involves representing others in legal matters.

5. True or False. The rule of client confidentiality applies only to lawyers, but as a professional, the paralegal voluntarily agrees to be bound by the rule.

6. A lawyer must
   a. keep a client reasonably informed about the status of the client's case.
   b. comply with a client's reasonable requests for information.
   c. explain things to the client so that the client can make informed decisions.
   d. none of the above
   e. all of the above

7. A Chinese Wall is established when
   a. the case is extremely sensitive and internal office confidentiality is necessary.
   b. isolation of a specific lawyer or a specific paralegal from all contacts in a case is necessary.
   c. isolation of sensitive information when confirmation to third parties that the client is being represented by the firm is necessary.
   d. a lawyer accepts a matter and he or she cannot contact the opposing party.

8. True or False. A lawyer never should give advice to an unrepresented person beyond the advice to obtain legal counsel.

9. True or False. All written or recorded communications soliciting employment from a prospective client known to be in need of legal services must include the term *Advertising Material* on the outside envelope or at the beginning and the end of recorded communications.

10. True or False. The duty of confidentiality applies during the period of representation but ends after the attorney-client relationship is terminated.

11. Contingency fees are prohibited in cases where
    a. a divorce will be granted.
    b. collection of debt is involved.
    c. a collection of support previously ordered has been granted and is now in default.
    d. private placement security transactions are involved.

12. Lawyers cannot
    a. enter into business ownership transactions with a client unless the terms are fair.
    b. prepare an instrument in which a client gives a lawyer or anyone related to the lawyer a gift, by will or otherwise, unless the client is related to the lawyer.
    c. represent adverse interests in the same case.
    d. b and c
    e. all of the above

13. True or False. A lawyer may accept a proprietary interest in the outcome of the case as payment of fees.

Use the following paragraph for Questions 14 through 17:

>*Charlie is a paralegal who is alone in his attorney-employer's office. The attorney is out of the city, and things are rather slow. A man calls the office seeking legal advice concerning a recent car accident. Charlie talks with the gentleman, gathers the details, and tells him the office will take the case. Charlie believes the attorney will be pleased with the new business. Pretending to be his employer, Charlie calls the opposing attorney to determine the status of the case. Before long, settlement discussions are taking place between Charlie and the opposing attorney.*

14. Based upon these facts, Charlie
    a. has committed several UPL violations.
    b. may be the subject of criminal charges.
    c. may be responsible for civil liability for damages incurred by the client.
    d. all of the above
    e. none of the above

15. True or False. Charlie was able to accept the case on behalf of the attorney.

16. True or False. While it was improper for Charlie to impersonate his employer, he did not violate any ethics rule.

17. True or False. Charlie's attorney may terminate Charlie immediately for a variety of reasons based on the facts.

18. Before most states issue a license to a lawyer to practice law, the applicant must demonstrate
    a. good moral character.
    b. graduation from an accredited law school.
    c. minimal competence by passing a state bar examination.
    d. a and c
    e. all of the above

19. True or False. Champerty is a proprietary interest in the outcome of a case.

20. A longtime client calls you and asks what the normal fee would be for a simple will. How should you reply?
    a. "The usual office charge is $85."
    b. "The fee varies from will to will, but Attorney Jones can determine that for you."
    c. "Paralegals cannot quote fees, but let me direct you to Attorney Jones."
    d. "The range for simple wills is $60 to $100."

21. True or False. A gratuitous client sends a mink jacket to a paralegal's home as a means of saying thank-you for all of the paralegal's hard work. It is permissible for the paralegal to accept the jacket.

22. True or False. If an administrative agency permits nonlawyer practice, a paralegal may establish a practice of exclusively representing clients before that agency.

23. A retainer is placed in a firm's trust account because an attorney is required to separate such funds according to
    a. banking rules.
    b. ethics rules.
    c. security rules.
    d. court rules.

24. True or False. Procrastination is permitted under the Model Rules as long as it is reasonable and justified.

25. True or False. Contingent fee arrangements must be reduced to writing through a retainer letter.

ANSWERS TO WEEK FIVE: COMMUNICATIONS WORKSHEET

1. gerund as object of sentence—The plaintiff maintains that the defendant admitted hitting plaintiff's car.
2. parallel construction; replace the semicolon with a comma—Since one who takes life too seriously often may be unhappy, **one** should maintain a good sense of humor.
3. wrong word—I am **averse** to this course of action.
4. add hyphen—The committee selected among four **well-considered** plans.
5. C
6. William asked, "Where are we going**?**"
7. C
8. pronoun agreement—An unabridged dictionary is very useful, but **it is** too heavy to take to school.
9. pronoun case—The lucky ones are **we**.
10. pronoun case—Do you think it could have been **he**?
11. pronoun case—**Who** did you say was coming?
12. wrong word (*presently* means "in the very near future")—It is Saturday, October 31.
13. add comma; consecutive adjectives—Please hand me the **little, brown** book.
14. misplaced modifier—We had final exams **only** last week.
15. no comma—The article "Watch Your Money" was written by Andrew Rush, Jr.
16. i
17. g
18. h
19. e
20. c
21. a
22. k
23. n
24. f
25. b

ANSWERS TO ETHICS QUIZ

1. e	14. d
2. d	15. False
3. True	16. False
4. True	17. True
5. False	18. e
6. e	19. True
7. b	20. c
8. True	21. False
9. True	22. True
10. False	23. b
11. a	24. False
12. e	25. True
13. False	

WEEK SIX: LITIGATION

LESSON PLAN

- Communications Worksheet (10 minutes); go over answers; students grade own
- Litigation (30 minutes); go over answers
- Encourage creation of time lines; instruct necessary skills

LITIGATION—GENERAL DESCRIPTION

Subtopics:

Jurisdiction and venue
Civil litigation process and rules
Civil discovery
Civil pleadings
Civil trial and appellate process and rules

SUGGESTED TEXT AND REFERENCES

Litigation

(*Note: Since court rules differ from state to state, all questions are based on the Federal Rules of Civil Procedure or on generally accepted practice and procedure.*)

Blanchard, Roderick, D., *Litigation and Trial Practice,* 6th Ed. (or most current), Delmar, Cengage Learning.

Federal Civil Judicial Procedure and Rules, 2012 Ed. (or most current), Thomson Reuters Westlaw (paperback).

Kane, Mary Kay, *Kane's Civil Procedure in a Nutshell,* 7th Ed., 2013, Thomson Reuters Westlaw.

Koerselman-Newman, Virginia, J. D., in cooperation with the National Association of Legal Assistants, Inc., *Certified Paralegal Review Manual: A Practical Guide to CP Exam Preparation,* 4th Ed., 2014, Delmar, Cengage Learning.

National Association of Legal Assistants, Inc., *NALA Manual for Paralegals and Legal Assistants,* 5th Ed., 2010, Delmar, Cengage Learning.

WEEK SIX: COMMUNICATIONS WORKSHEET

Make corrections as necessary to the following sentences. Write "C" in front of those sentences that are correct as written.

1. More than half of all women over the age of thirty-five have not finished high school in this country.

2. The students mistook the teacher to be me.

3. The doctor was thought to be she.

4. Who among us have never failed?

5. Precise-writing skills are essential for every paralegal.

6. Courtney wore a scarlet red suit for the job interview.

7. Raymond thought the thief to be she.

8. When I finished the test, I knew that I did well, and I was pleased.

9. My husband Ken is an avid golfer.

10. We go to Reno each March, it has become a tradition.

11. Everywhere we go, people think that she is I.

12. It has been a long eventful year.

13. The speaker was thought to be he.

14. Practice tests are generally helpful in preparing for the Certified Paralegal Examination.

15. Please come to the Ozarks with Louise and I.

Match each term in the left column with the most correct definition or synonym from the right column.

16. _____ empirical
17. _____ rancor
18. _____ enigmatic
19. _____ filial
20. _____ placid
21. _____ rapacious
22. _____ jettison
23. _____ onerous
24. _____ opprobrium
25. _____ encomium

a. discard, throw overboard
b. of a brother or a sister
c. formal expression of praise
d. disgrace, reproach
e. oppressive, burdensome
f. of a son or daughter
g. derived from observation
h. calm, serene
i. puzzling
j. anger, spite
k. vesture
l. marauding, predatory

LITIGATION QUIZ

Choose the most correct answer.

1. True or False. Formal discovery cannot be conducted before a civil complaint is filed.

2. True or False. Juries may decide issues related to both law and fact in simple cases.

3. True or False. The basic pleadings in a federal civil case include the complaint, the answer, and the reply.

4. True or False. A permissive counterclaim is one that requires the court's permission before it can be filed in a civil case.

5. True or False. It is unethical for a lawyer knowingly to offer evidence during litigation that he or she knows is prejudicial.

6. When a case is appealed, the appellate court will base its decision on
    a. the credibility of the witnesses.
    b. the record of the lower court.
    c. reevaluation of the facts presented to the jury.
    d. none of the above

7. If a paralegal is instructed to ensure that a particular witness personally appears and brings specific documents with him or her, which of the following should be issued?
    a. summons
    b. subpoena
    c. subpoena duces tecum
    d. subpoena capias

8. If a person fails to answer interrogatories within the time specified, which rule of the Federal Rules of Civil Procedure provides the remedy for this failure?
    a. Rule 33
    b. Rule 34
    c. Rule 36
    d. Rule 37

9. True or False. A civil action is commenced in federal court when the defendant is served with a summons and a copy of the complaint.

10. When computing the deadline for response,
    a. include the day of service.
    b. count only ordinary working days.
    c. exclude the day of service.
    d. schedule it for Friday if the last day falls on Saturday.

11. A plaintiff is required to respond to a counterclaim
    a. ten days from date of service.
    b. twenty days from date of service.
    c. thirty days from date of service.
    d. only if he or she denies the allegations.

12. True or False. A federal court summons is issued by the plaintiff's attorney and may be served by the U.S. Marshal's Office.

13. True or False. An attorney may issue a subpoena to a witness in a federal civil action.

14. True or False. A major advantage of interrogatories is that they can be used to obtain background information from nonparty eyewitnesses; the information then can be used to prepare for their subsequent depositions.

15. True or False. Proximate cause is involved when the term *sine qua non* is used.

16. True or False. Loss of companionship is classified as general damages in a personal injury case.

17. True or False. A party may waive personal jurisdiction but cannot waive subject matter jurisdiction.

18. True or False. A cross-claim must arise out of the same events or occurrence as the original complaint.

19. An interlocutory appeal must be filed
    a. ten days after entry of the interlocutory order.
    b. twenty days after entry of the interlocutory order.
    c. thirty days after entry of the interlocutory order.
    d. forty-five days after entry of the interlocutory order.

20. Proper venue for a federal civil action is where
    1. all plaintiffs reside.
    2. all defendants reside.
    3. the cause of action arose.
    4. the defendants are subject to service of process.
    5. all of the above

    a. 1, 2, and 3
    b. 2, 3, and 4
    c. 1, 3, and 5
    d. 5

Match each term in the left column with the most correct definition or synonym from the right column. No item is used twice.

21. _____ caveat
22. _____ ex post facto
23. _____ et ux
24. _____ in loco parentis
25. _____ scintilla
26. _____ inter alia
27. _____ non obstante
28. _____ nolle prosequi
29. _____ inter se
30. _____ scienter

a. among other things
b. notwithstanding
c. let the buyer beware
d. among themselves
e. beware, warning
f. after the fact
g. knowingly
h. and wife
i. in place of a parent
j. cause to know, give notice
k. the least particle, a spark
l. unwilling to prosecute

ANSWERS TO WEEK SIX: COMMUNICATIONS WORKSHEET

1. where did they attend?—More than half of all women over the age of thirty-five **in this country** have not finished high school.
2. C
3. C
4. verb agreement—Who among us **has** never failed?
5. no hyphen—**Precise writing** skills are essential for every paralegal.
6. C
7. pronoun case—Raymond thought the thief to be **her**.
8. past perfect case; completed in the past before some other past act—When I finished the test, I knew that I **had done** well, and I was pleased.
9. add commas—My husband, **Ken,** is an avid golfer.
10. comma splice—use semicolon—We go to Reno each **March;** it has become a tradition.
11. C
12. consecutive adjectives; use comma—It has been a **long, eventful** year.
13. C
14. C
15. pronoun case—Please come to the Ozarks with Louise and **me**.
16. g
17. j
18. i
19. f
20. h
21. l
22. a
23. e
24. d
25. c

ANSWERS TO LITIGATION QUIZ

1. False	9. False	17. True	25. k
2. False	10. c	18. True	26. a
3. True	11. d	19. a	27. b
4. False	12. False	20. b	28. l
5. False	13. True	21. e	29. d
6. b	14. False	22. f	30. g
7. c	15. True	23. h	
8. d	16. False	24. i	

WEEK SEVEN: CONTRACTS

LESSON PLAN

- Communications Worksheet (10 minutes); go over answers; students grade own
- Contracts (35 minutes); go over answers

CONTRACTS—GENERAL DESCRIPTION

Subtopics:

Contract classifications
Contract formation
Contract defenses
Contract remedies

SUGGESTED TEXT AND REFERENCES

Contracts

(*Note: Most college business law texts contain excellent materials in this area.*)

Frey, Martin and Frey, Phyllis Hurley, *Introduction to the Law of Contracts*, 4th Ed. (or most current), 2008, Delmar, Cengage Learning.

Koerselman-Newman, Virginia, J. D., in cooperation with the National Association of Legal Assistants, Inc., *Certified Paralega Review Manual: A Practical Guide to CP Exam Preparation*, 4th Ed., 2014, Delmar, Cengage Learning.

Rohwer, Claude and Skrocki, Anthony, *Contracts in a Nutshell*, 7th Ed. (or most current), 2010, Thomson Reuters Westlaw.

WEEK SEVEN: COMMUNICATIONS WORKSHEET

Make corrections as necessary to the following sentences. Write "C" in front of those sentences that are correct as written.

1. People who buy handguns with criminal intent will find a way to obtain guns, whether it is legal or not.

2. I am anxious to earn my Certified Paralegal designation.

3. Dan did a credible job of summarizing the depositions.

4. My parents did not like me getting home after midnight.

5. To read classical books and watching public television are helpful in gaining a broad education.

6. When depressed, a church is a good place to go.

7. Study for the Certified Paralegal exam can be accomplished by anyone who has acquired superior communication skills in two months.

8. Everyone must assert their rights if we are to gain the dean's attention.

9. I became more and more discouraged, all I wanted was to go home.

10. We need to carefully plan for the project's success.

11. The news came to me about my brother's illness in a letter.

12. Paralegals are capable of interviewing clients, performing legal research, and can implement discovery plans.

13. The deceased revised her will at least four times.

14. In need of repair, Julie bought the sofa at a reasonable price.

15. William made a favorable first impression.

Match each term in the left column with the most correct definition or synonym from the right column.

16. _____ lugubrious	a.	sudden, illogical change
17. _____ nebulous	b.	extraordinary, huge
	c.	worldly, nonspiritual
18. _____ millennium	d.	crack, crevice
19. _____ umbrage	e.	explosive, volatile
	f.	mournful, sad
20. _____ prodigious	g.	temporary
21. _____ abjure	h.	renounce, disavow
	i.	future perfection in the world
22. _____ sanguine	j.	vague
23. _____ capricious	k.	offense, resentment
	l.	hopeful
24. _____ temporal		
25. _____ fissure		

CONTRACTS QUIZ

Choose the most correct answer.

1. True or False. A contract may be both written and expressed, but may not be both oral and implied.

2. True or False. Under the UCC, the offeree must accept in writing.

3. True or False. Under the UCC, parties can modify terms of a contract without new consideration.

4. True or False. If a contract for sale of goods fails to state the terms of payment, the UCC provides rules to establish payment terms.

5. Forcing a party to enter into a contract under fear of threats is called
   a. duress.
   b. undue influence.
   c. deception.
   d. unilateral mistake of fact.

6. Miller owns a farm. He contemplates the following contracts. Which of these must be in writing under the Statute of Frauds?
   a. a sale of pigs for $400
   b. a contract in which Miller agrees to harvest his neighbor's wheat crop for a payment of $750
   c. a lease of a parcel of land to James for six months
   d. an easement to James for $5,000

7. The parole evidence rule applies to exclude evidence to modify a(n)
   a. clear and complete written contract.
   b. clear and complete oral contract.
   c. quasi contract.
   d. ambiguous written contract.

8. The rule by which a third party has no right to sue on a contract to which he or she is not a party is called
   a. assignment.
   b. delegation.
   c. anticipatory repudiation.
   d. privity of contract.

9. Jill tells her stockbroker to buy 500 shares of Apex stock if it drops to $50 a share within the next 15 days. Jill's instructions are a
   a. concurrent condition.
   b. condition subsequent.
   c. condition precedent.
   d. constructive condition.

10. Jack disputes a $500 dental bill. After Jack discusses the matter with his dentist, they agree that Jack will pay $375 in full settlement of the debt. When the money is paid, this compromise will be called a(n)
    a. accord and satisfaction.
    b. novation.
    c. modification.
    d. delegation.

11. True or False. The beneficiary of a life insurance policy owned by another is called a donee beneficiary.

12. True or False. Under the UCC, minerals are classified as goods if they are extracted by the buyer.

13. True or False. Sales contracts must cover present transfers for goods already in existence.

14. True or False. Coal is an example of fungible goods.

15. Yarn Notions, a manufacturer, ships 100 scarf kits to Yarn Barn, a retailer. Both companies have agreed that Yarn Barn may select any or all of the kits for resale to customers, with any unsold kits to be returned in six weeks. Two weeks after Yarn Barn receives the kits, a fire destroys all of them. The risk of loss rests with
    a. Yarn Notions because the sale to Yarn Barn is not final.
    b. Yarn Notions because Yarn Barn has not accepted the kits.
    c. Yarn Barn because it accepted the kits.
    d. Yarn Barn because title and risk of loss have passed to it.

16. Andrew purchases a drill press from White & Ducker Tools. The drill does not work properly, and Andrew demands his money back. He seeks the remedy of
    a. reformation.
    b. rescission.
    c. specific performance.
    d. compensatory damages.

17. Generally speaking, title to goods sold under a shipment contract passes when the
    a. goods are identified to the contract.
    b. seller puts the goods in the hands of a carrier.
    c. carrier delivers the goods to the buyer.
    d. buyer obtains insurance.

18. True or False. Quantum meruit is an equitable remedy.

19. True or False. If no time for acceptance is stated in the offer, the offer terminates automatically at the end of ninety days.

20. True or False. A counteroffer acts as a rejection of the original offer.

Match each term in the left column with the most correct definition or synonym from the right column. No item is used twice.

21. _____ videlicet (viz.)
22. _____ sua sponte
23. _____ in pari delicto
24. _____ sui juris
25. _____ pur autre vie
26. _____ nul tort
27. _____ onus probandi
28. _____ erratum
29. _____ sui generic
30. _____ ore tenus

a. voluntarily
b. by word of mouth, verbally
c. that is to say, namely
d. burden of proof
e. of its own kind or class
f. as if it were
g. for (during) the life of another
h. in equal fault
i. in his own right
j. no wrong done
k. by itself, taken alone
l. error

ANSWERS TO WEEK SEVEN: COMMUNICATIONS WORKSHEET

1. poorly written; verbose—People with criminal intent will find a way to obtain guns, whether it is legal or not.
2. word usage—I am **eager** to earn my Certified Paralegal designation.
3. word usage—Dan did a **creditable** job of summarizing the depositions.
4. possessive pronoun—My parents did not like **my** getting home after midnight.
5. parallel construction—**Reading** classical books and watching public television are helpful in gaining a broad education.
6. misplaced modifier—**A** church is a good place to go **when a person is depressed.**
7. misplaced modifier—Study for the Certified Paralegal Examination can be accomplished **in two months** by anyone who has acquired superior communication skills.
8. pronoun agreement—Everyone must assert **his or her** rights if we are to gain the dean's attention.
9. use a semicolon instead of a comma—I became more and more **discouraged; all** I wanted was to go home.
10. split infinitive—We need to plan **carefully** for the project's success.
11. misplaced modifier—The news about my brother's illness **came to me** in a letter.
12. parallel construction—Paralegals are capable of interviewing clients, performing legal research, and **implementing** discovery plans.
13. word usage—The **testatrix** revised her will at least four times.
14. misplaced modifier—Julie bought the sofa, **in need of repair,** at a reasonable price.
15. C
16. f
17. j
18. i
19. k
20. b
21. h
22. l
23. a
24. c
25. d

ANSWERS TO CONTRACTS QUIZ

1. True
2. False
3. True
4. True
5. a
6. d
7. a
8. d
9. c
10. a
11. True
12. False
13. False
14. True
15. b

16. b
17. b
18. True
19. False
20. True
21. c
22. a
23. h
24. i
25. g
26. j
27. d
28. l
29. e
30. b

WEEK EIGHT: BUSINESS ORGANIZATIONS

LESSON PLAN

- Communications Worksheet (10 minutes); go over answers; students grade own
- Business Organizations Quiz (30 minutes); go over answers

BUSINESS ORGANIZATIONS—GENERAL DESCRIPTION

Subtopics:

Corporations
Publicly-held corporations
Partnerships and limited liability companies (LLCs)
Other business entities
Financial structure and management of business entities

SUGGESTED TEXT AND REFERENCES

Business Organizations

(***Note:*** *Most college business law texts have excellent materials.*)

Jentz, Gaylord A., and Miller, Roger, LeRoy, *Business Law Today*, 8th Ed., 2009, Cengage South-Western.

Hamilton, Robert W., and Freer, Richard D., *The Law of Corporations in a Nutshell,* 6th Ed. (or most current), 2011, Thomson Reuters Westlaw.

Koerselman-Newman, Virginia, J. D., in cooperation with the National Association of Legal Assistants, Inc., *Certified Paralegal Review Manual: A Practical Guide to CP Exam Preparation*, 4th Ed., 2014, Delmar, Cengage Learning.

Moye, John E., *The Law of Business Organizations*, 6th Ed. (or most current), 2005, Delmar, Cengage Learning.

Schneeman, Angela, *The Law of Corporations and Other Business Organizations*, 6th Ed. (or most current), 2013, Delmar, Cengage Learning.

WEEK EIGHT: COMMUNICATIONS WORKSHEET

Make corrections as necessary to the following sentences. Write "C" in front of those sentences that are correct as written.

1. A large amount of students missed the first day of class.

2. Laying on the beach is Bill's favorite pastime.

3. Amy said, "Hand me the envelope marked urgent."

4. Leisure time is a product of the Twentieth Century.

5. If Raymond was asleep, he did not see the eclipse of the moon.

6. I witnessed many events by the time I retired.

7. I cannot hear anything because of him snoring.

8. If Marie continues, she will help many people by the time she retires from nursing.

9. This is she on the telephone.

10. Bill and me want you to join us for dinner.

11. An organization is only as strong as their members.

12. Only two people, him and her, left early.

13. When it comes to Ruth and me, nothing can stop us.

14. We do not know whom the president will select.

15. I knew that dinner was burned by the odor.

Match each term in the left column with the most correct definition or synonym from the right column.

16. _____ somnambulist	a.	misleading, incorrect
17. _____ ebullient	b.	instructive, contains lessons
18. _____ stentorian	c.	sleep walker
19. _____ diaphanous	d.	inclined to silence
20. _____ dilettante	e.	timid, shy
21. _____ soporific	f.	bubbly, effervescent
22. _____ didactic	g.	an amateur, a dabbler
23. _____ specious	h.	anathema
24. _____ reticent	i.	causing drowsiness
25. _____ diffident	j.	exceptionally loud
	k.	anomaly
	l.	transparent

BUSINESS ORGANIZATIONS QUIZ

Choose the most correct answer.

1. The most common form of business organization is the
    a. closely held corporation.
    b. limited partnership.
    c. general partnership.
    d. sole proprietorship.

2. General partnerships are governed by the
    a. Model Partnership Act.
    b. Revised Uniform Limited Partnership Act.
    c. Uniform Partnership Act.
    d. Model Business Organization Act.

3. A de facto corporation is
    a. not a corporation at all because of failure to comply with statutory organizational requirements.
    b. a corporation that has complied with all statutory organizational requirements.
    c. a corporation that has insufficient capital.
    d. a corporation that has limited the personal liability of the shareholders.

4. The owners of equity securities are called
    a. equity holders or bondholders.
    b. shareholders or stockholders.
    c. capitalists.
    d. debenture holders.

5. The articles of incorporation may provide that shares of a given class can be converted into shares of another class on some predetermined ratio. These shares are known as
    a. redeemable shares.
    b. preferred shares.
    c. outstanding shares.
    d. convertible shares.

6. Preemptive rights are exercised when a shareholder has the right
    a. of first refusal to purchase any additional shares of the corporation.
    b. to convert common stock to preferred stock on a predetermined date.
    c. to purchase a proportionate share of a new issue of common stock before it is offered for sale to others.
    d. to purchase shares of a new issue of common stock for a price less than market value.
    e. all of the above
    f. none of the above

7. Before or while the corporation is being organized, a method for acquiring investment capital is through
    a. stock options.
    b. stock warrants.
    c. stock rights.
    d. stock subscriptions.

8. A limited partner
    a.   may participate only in the management of the business.
    b.   may contribute to the partnership only with cash or property.
    c.   has no liability for debts or loss beyond his or her investment contribution.
    d.   cannot be both the general partner and a limited partner.
    e.   all of the above

9. A joint venture is
    a.   two or more individuals merging efforts for one event only.
    b.   an endeavor of two or more persons who intend to have an ongoing business relationship.
    c.   created by a government entity to administer government purposes.
    d.   an artificial entity created by state statute for two or more persons to carry on a specific business or activity.

10. A written proxy
    a.   grants authority to another person to vote at a directors' meeting.
    b.   grants only specific authority to vote on a designated matter.
    c.   may grant general authority to vote on all matters at a stockholders' meeting.
    d.   cannot be revoked for six months once given to the designated proxy holder.
    e.   none of the above

Select the worst answer for each of the following questions.

11. Most states have securities statutes known as blue sky laws. These statutes were adopted to
    a.   prevent fraud by unscrupulous promoters selling worthless securities.
    b.   require registration of securities brokers and dealers.
    c.   promote insider trading between stockholders.
    d.   register all securities traded in the state.

12. When two corporations merge,
    a.   the corporations dissolve and a new corporation is created.
    b.   creditor's rights are unaffected.
    c.   a plan of merger is approved by each corporation's board of directors.
    d.   the stockholders of each corporation approve the plan of merger.

13. The corporate officer's express authority to act for the corporation derives from
    a.   state corporation statutes.
    b.   the articles of incorporation.
    c.   the bylaws.
    d.   resolutions of the board of directors.
    e.   none of the above
    f.   all of the above

14. Under the charter option statutes, a director's liability may be limited by the corporation's articles of incorporation for any act or omission except
    a.   intentional harm to the corporation or stockholders.
    b.   improper distributions of dividends or stock.
    c.   deliberate criminal violations.
    d.   unbiased mistakes or errors.

15. A voting trust
    a. may control large blocks of stock.
    b. is created by a group of shareholders transferring legal title to a trustee.
    c. may allow the trustee to vote the shares, subject to any trust restrictions.
    d. controls the shares and voting rights indefinitely.

Select the best answer for each of the following questions.

16. True or False. S corporations may have forty shareholders.

17. True or False. Double taxation occurs when corporate profits are taxed at corporate rates, distributions are made to the shareholders as dividends, and the dividends are taxed again to the shareholders at the individual income tax rate.

18. True or False. Noncumulative preferred stock receives dividends for all years before dividends are paid to common stockholders.

19. True or False. Stock splits reduce the price per share.

20. True or False. A promoter is one who develops a business idea, arranges for capital, and acquires assets for the corporation before the corporation is actually organized.

21. True or False. A limited liability company is a hybrid of a corporation and a partnership.

22. True or False. One advantage of a sole proprietorship is having the profits taxed at individual tax rates.

23. True or False. A general partnership must have as one of its business purposes the intention to generate profit.

24. True or False. A general partnership must file a partnership income tax return and pay its own tax separately.

25. Treasury stock
    a. is a class of stock permitted by specific authority of the articles of incorporation.
    b. has no voting rights.
    c. has preemptive rights.
    d. is entitled to dividends.

26. Sally owns 500 shares of Fix-it Corporation. At the annual shareholders' meeting, five directors are to be elected. If Sally wishes to exercise her cumulative voting rights, what is the largest number of votes she can cast for any one director?
    a. 500
    b. 2,500
    c. 2,000
    d. 1,000

27. Daffy and Bugs form a partnership. Daffy contributes $20,000 to the partnership, and Bugs contributes 30,000 pounds of carrots having a value of $10,000. At year's end, there is a profit of $15,000. No agreement was made between the parties for distribution of the profits. How much will each partner receive?
    a. Daffy will receive $10,000; Bugs, $5,000.
    b. Daffy will receive $5,000.
    c. Daffy will receive $5,000; Bugs, $2,500.
    d. none of the above

28. Bugs, Elmer Fudd, and Porky form a limited partnership called Carrots and Spuds, a Limited Partnership. Bugs is the general partner, and Elmer and Porky are limited partners. Elmer becomes disenchanted with Bugs's managerial skill because of his laid-back attitude. Toting his shotgun on his shoulder, Elmer stomps his way to headquarters. Upon his arrival, he announces his presence with an authoritative knock. When Bugs opens the door, Elmer enters, pushing Bugs aside. At that point, Elmer declares through the sites of his trusty shotgun, "Th-th-this is a management takeover. S-s-step aside, Wabbit!" Under the Uniform Limited Partnership Act, Elmer cannot become the new general partner under the existing agreement because
    a. Elmer did not have Porky's approval to name a new manager and general partner.
    b. limited partners may not participate in the management or control of the business, with or without a gun.
    c. the general partner (Bugs) is the only agent for service of process within the state.
    d. none of the above

29. Because of the altercation with Elmer, Bugs decides to leave Carrots and Spuds, a Limited Partnership, to look for employment where he will be appreciated. There are no provisions for a successor general partner in the limited partnership agreement. Porky refuses to continue the business with Elmer even though Elmer is willing to take on the responsibilities of general partner, but now there are no partners. What will become of the limited partnership?
    a. Elmer will need to find new partners.
    b. The partnership will dissolve because of the withdrawal of the general partner.
    c. The partnership may continue with only Elmer serving as both the general and limited partner.
    d. none of the above

ANSWERS TO WEEK EIGHT: COMMUNICATIONS WORKSHEET

1. word usage—A large **number** of students missed the first day of class.
2. word usage—**Lying** on the beach is Bill's favorite pastime.
3. punctuation—Amy said, "Hand me the envelope marked '**urgent**.' "
4. capitalization—Leisure time is a product of the **twentieth century**.
5. C
6. past event occurring prior to another past event—I **had** witnessed many events by the time I retired.
7. possessive case—I cannot hear anything because of **his** snoring.
8. future perfect—If Marie continues, she will **have helped** many people by the time she retires from nursing.
9. C
10. pronoun case—Bill and **I** want you to join us for dinner.
11. agreement—An organization is only as strong as **its** members.
12. nominative case—Only two people, **he** and **she**, left early.
13. C
14. C
15. misplaced modifier—I knew **by the odor** that dinner was burned.
16. c
17. f
18. j
19. l
20. g
21. i
22. b
23. a
24. d
25. e

ANSWERS TO BUSINESS ORGANIZATIONS QUIZ

1.	d	16.	True
2.	c	17.	True
3.	a	18.	False
4.	b	19.	True
5.	d	20.	True
6.	c	21.	True
7.	d	22.	True
8.	c	23.	True
9.	a	24.	False
10.	c	25.	b
11.	c	26.	b
12.	a	27.	d—both will get $7,500
13.	e	28.	b
14.	d	29.	b
15.	d		

WEEK NINE:
MOCK EXAMINATION

LESSON PLAN

- A three-hour overall time limit
- Sections taken in succession under established time limits; answers are provided at the end of this class session (students grade their own at home)
- Students must preregister for the four substantive law sections they wish to take

TAKING A TEST—HELPFUL HINTS

The following suggestions are taken from the *Certified Paralegal Review Manual: A Practical Guide to CP Exam Preparation*, by Virginia Koerselman-Newman, J. D., in cooperation with the National Association of Legal Assistants, Inc., 4th Ed., 2014, Delmar, Cengage Learning.

Prepare Yourself

- If possible, travel to the testing site the day before the examination is to be taken. Determine the best route to take and estimate the time to arrive there. Allow for morning rush-hour traffic and plan to arrive twenty to thirty minutes ahead of time. Determine where you will park and how much it will cost. Familiarize yourself with the location of the testing room and of the other facilities located in the building, such as the restroom(s), snack bar or coffee shop, if any, and so forth.
- On the evening before the examination, review your outlines and notes one last time for the sections to be administered the next day. Then put them away.
- Get a good night's rest. You will need all of your energy when the test begins. Don't squander it by sitting up half the night, worrying about what will happen tomorrow or trying to cram. Cramming at the last minute will do nothing but cause confusion and panic. Don't do it.
- Relax. Immediately before the exam begins, panic can immobilize you unless you stay in control. Before entering the examination room, walk around and stretch your neck, shoulders, arms, hands, and legs. Don't just pace.
- In selecting your examination seat, sit where you can hear the examination administrator without being distracted by activity at or near his or her desk. If possible, avoid those seats located near air vents.
- Breathe deeply—breathe in through the nose, bringing the air all the way down to the knees, and hold it for a count of five; then breathe out through the mouth s-l-o-w-l-y until all of the air is released. Continue this exercise until the air comes out slowly and smoothly.
- If you begin to panic while taking the exam, (evidenced by the inability to think clearly—you see the words, but they don't register in your head) stop and quietly perform the breathing exercise. As you breathe in, imagine yourself going down an elevator all the way to the lower subbasement. Stay at that level for a count of five and then slowly breathe out as you return to ground level. Do it again. Then go back to work. This thirty-second exercise is well worth the time invested.

Test Questions in General

- All test questions are designed within a national framework. Do not rely on the rules of a specific state when answering any of the questions.
- Answer all questions, even if you have to guess. Since there is no additional penalty for a wrong answer, guessing may result in a few extra points here and there. An unanswered question, however, never can be correct.
- Read the instructions for each group of questions very carefully. Be absolutely certain that you know what you are being asked to do before you begin.

- Be sure that you understand each question before you attempt to answer it. Read it twice if necessary. Fine-line distinctions are commonly drawn in examinations like this one. If you read a question too quickly, important words will be overlooked.
- Read the question as it is, not as you expected it to be. Don't try to help the question-writer by qualifying your answer. The question means exactly what it says.
- Pace yourself in relation to the length of the examination section. Answer the questions you know first. Write the question number of the others on your scratch paper and come back to them later. Don't spend too much time on any one question.
- Do not change your answers unless you are positive that you wrote the wrong answer the first time. If you read the question carefully, your first impulse is almost always right. If you second-guess yourself, the second guess likely will be wrong.
- If you finish the section before the allotted time has expired, stop. Do not go back through the questions, because second-guessing problems will arise (see above).
- Use the break between each testing period effectively. Walk, stretch, relax, and mentally prepare yourself for the upcoming testing period. Do not squander this valuable time by dwelling on the section that you just finished. It is over. Move on.
- Resist the temptation to compare your answers with those of other applicants while on break, during lunch, or at the end of the day. Do not even listen to this type of discussion while sections remain to be taken. Politely excuse yourself if anyone else talks about specific answers. If any of their answers were different from yours (and some of them will be different), it will create unnecessary anxiety, which, in turn, will have a negative effect on your performance during the next testing period.

True or False Questions

- Be wary of true or false questions that contain the words *always* or *never*. While there are occasional exceptions, few things in the law are "always true" or "never true."
- If any part of the statement is inaccurate or incorrect, the entire statement is incorrect, in which case the answer is "false."
- The words *generally* or *may* in a true-false question often indicates that the answer is true.

Multiple-Choice Questions

- Read the questions carefully. Multiple-choice questions generally will ask you to select the most correct answer or the best answer, but some will ask you to select the least correct answer or the worst answer. Watch for these.
- Beware of "none of the above" and "all of the above" selections. Certainly there are some questions for which "none" or "all" is the correct answer. As a general rule, these questions are few.
- If a question or a set of answers sounds totally foreign, leave that question and go on to those you can answer. Remember to write the question number on your scratch paper. If you return to the question and still do not know the answer, guess. There is no penalty for wrong answers, so there is no benefit in leaving any question unanswered.
- Make an educated guess or use a process of elimination. Eliminate as many of the wrong selections as you can and then pick from the remaining selections. If your instincts point to one of them, choose it and move on to another question.
- If you cannot make even an educated guess about the correct answer and if you have not already eliminated the "c" selection as being wrong, "c" is the best guess (based upon generic testing statistics). Although the "a" selection is sometimes the correct answer for a particular question, it is the worst guess statistically. Comparing statistics and educated guesses, your educated guess is always the better choice.

Matching Questions

- Read the instructions to determine whether items from either list can be used more than once. If not, the items can be matched through a process of elimination. Match those that you know are correct and select the others by eliminating those that you know are wrong.
- Matching questions tend to take more time than either true-false or multiple-choice questions. Budget your time with this in mind.

Essay Questions

- Quickly skim the instructions and the question to get a feel for the material. Then read them again, very carefully this time. With this reading, underline any important points or items. This makes it easier to find things later, which saves time.
- Be absolutely sure you understand what it is that you are to do (whether it is to summarize, to compare, to discuss, and so forth).
- If you are asked to summarize material, condense it to the bare-bones facts. Do not editorialize; do not change facts or add facts that are not clearly stated in the original material. In general, a summary should be no longer than one-fourth the length of the original material. Double-check to be certain that the names, places, times, and so forth, in your summary coincide with the original material.
- If you are asked to compare one thing with another, limit the essay to comparison and contrast (similarities and differences). Don't engage in extraneous dissertations. For instance, do not explain how a particular concept or principle evolved historically when the question asks simply that you compare it with another specified concept or principle.
- When asked to explain or to discuss an issue, concept, term, or the like, do precisely that. At a minimum, the discussion must provide a concise definition. It may also include usage—when, how, and why it is used. Do not compare it with something else unless that is the only way to explain it, which rarely will be the case.
- Do not define terms by using those same terms as part of the definition. In other words, do not say "Criminal law is the law that defines criminal conduct." This is a circular statement. It defines nothing and no points could be given for it.
- Do not ask rhetorical questions in an essay answer. For example, do not ask, "Why have the rule if it is not enforced?" Rephrase the thought into a declarative statement, such as, "The rule means nothing if it is not enforced."
- Plan to spend at least as much time thinking about and planning your answer as you spend writing it.
- Use the scratch paper provided to you to plan your answer completely before typing anything in the text box. Do not merely begin to type, believing (or hoping) that you can clarify your thoughts as you progress. It almost never works.
- Get to the point. In planning your answer, type the three or four (three is better) most important points to be made. Then put them in complete sentences; be sure they convey complete thoughts and make sense. Use abbreviations and brief forms of words to speed the process. Once you have done this, number them in the logical order in which they should be presented or discussed. Decide whether there are any subpoints that must be included for clarity. If so, jot a word or a phrase under the main point as a reminder. Unless the subpoint is absolutely necessary, leave it out.
- Formulate a brief, introductory sentence and draft the final answer. Stick to your planned outline. To the extent that you digress, your answer will appear disjointed and disorganized.
- Say what you need to say in as few words as possible and then stop. Refer to the Communications section of the *Certified Paralegal Review Manual* for more information.
- Double-check spelling, punctuation, grammar, and word usage. Make corrections as needed. Errors can result in lost points.

- Do not attempt to divert the graders' attention by bluffing or by discussing peripheral issues at length. This technique does not work and can backfire in such a way that the resulting essay score is less than it would have been if the applicant had stopped at those things that were known and were relevant to the question.
- Do not try to be humorous; it generates no points. Likewise, do not write explanatory or apologetic notes to the grader. It's unprofessional.

PART
3

Certified Paralegal Program Mock Examination

Examination Sections and Time Limits

Communications	**20 minutes**
Judgment and Analytical Ability	**25 minutes**
Ethics	**15 minutes**
Legal Research	**20 minutes**
Substantive Law	**40 minutes**

COMMUNICATIONS

Select the best answer for each of the following questions unless a specific group of questions instructs you to do otherwise.

1. Neither the firefighters nor the union (was) (were) prepared to compromise.

2. Hard work is essential to (insure) (ensure) a passing score on the exam.

3. Without discipline from parents, good manners (allude) (elude) most children.

4. We felt (bad) (badly) about being late for class every week.

5. (Most) (Mostly) lawyers are frustrated actors.

6. The reason I became a paralegal was because I found the law interesting, but I did not want to become a lawyer.
   a. The sentence contains faulty punctuation.
   b. The sentence contains faulty grammar.
   c. The sentence is verbose.
   d. The sentence is correct.

7. Listening to carols and baking cookies, which we did each year as children, is an important part of our holiday tradition.
   a. The sentence contains faulty punctuation.
   b. The sentence contains faulty grammar.
   c. The sentence is verbose.
   d. The sentence is correct.

8. I did not realize how much weight Bill gained until I saw him at the courthouse yesterday.
   a. The sentence contains faulty punctuation.
   b. The sentence contains faulty grammar.
   c. The sentence is verbose.
   d. The sentence is correct.

9. My friend, Larry, considers himself a connoisseur of fine wines.
   a. The sentence contains faulty punctuation.
   b. The sentence contains faulty grammar.
   c. The sentence is verbose.
   d. The sentence is correct.

10. Were you there when Jane said, "I hope they fire that idiot"?
    a. The sentence contains faulty punctuation.
    b. The sentence contains faulty grammar.
    c. The sentence is verbose.
    d. The sentence is correct.

11. Julia's art collection contains the most unique array of color, texture, and design that I ever have seen.
    a. The sentence contains faulty punctuation.
    b. The sentence contains faulty grammar.
    c. The sentence is verbose.
    d. The sentence is correct.

12. The judge snarled, "For the last time, you must speak louder".
    a. The sentence contains faulty punctuation.
    b. The sentence contains faulty grammar.
    c. The sentence is verbose.
    d. The sentence is correct.

13. Ruth always takes a large, leather briefcase home for the weekend; but she never seems to catch up with her work.
    a. The sentence contains faulty punctuation.
    b. The sentence contains faulty grammar.
    c. The sentence is verbose.
    d. The sentence is correct.

14. When the meeting was finished, I went to the closest door marked "Exit"; but it had been locked from the outside, and I could not open it.
    a. The sentence contains faulty punctuation.
    b. The sentence contains faulty grammar.
    c. The sentence is verbose.
    d. The sentence is correct.

15. Although our client may not agree, it seems abundantly clear that he has some liability in this case.
    a. The sentence contains faulty punctuation.
    b. The sentence contains faulty grammar.
    c. The sentence is verbose.
    d. The sentence is correct.

16. We cannot _____ social change unless we begin with our own attitudes.
    a. affect
    b. effect

17. An attorney must know all of the relevant facts before she can _____ her client concerning his options.
    a. advise
    b. inform

18. Linguistics _____ a difficult field of study.
    a. are
    b. is

19. _____ of the lawyers was opposed to the change.
    a. Every one
    b. Everyone

20. None of the windows _____ open when I arrived.
    a. was
    b. were

Some of the following sentences contain a grammar error. Some are verbose. No sentence contains more than one error. Choose your answer by circling either "a" if the sentence is verbose or contains faulty grammar or "b" if the sentence contains neither type of error.

21. To thoroughly understand the problem, one must be aware of all of the facts.
    a.
    b.

22. We must interview all witnesses before we will be able to consider the matter fully.
    a.
    b.

23. The photocopy machine is not working like it should.
    a.
    b.

24. Everyone entering her home must take their shoes off.
    a.
    b.

25. Please have this project reviewed by whoever has the time to do it.
    a.
    b.

26. The fact that he studied hard for the examination probably had some bearing on his good grade.
    a.
    b.

27. Who do you think will be selected from among the applicants?
    a.
    b.

28. Neither of the attorneys were willing to compromise.
    a.
    b.

29. He has passed the examination because he studied very hard.
    a.
    b.

30. Bill could not bear to listen to David complaining every day.
    a.
    b.

The following sentences may contain an error in grammar, word usage, or punctuation. Some sentences are correct. No sentence contains more than one error. Select the underlined part that must be changed to correct the sentence. If there is no error, select "e."

31. Jim carries a <u>little, brown book</u> with <u>him everywhere he</u> <u>goes and writes</u> down
            a   b   c

    the name of each new <u>person whom he</u> meets. <u>No error.</u>
                              d   e

    a.
    b.
    c.
    d.
    e.

32. My <u>father Fred</u> <u>has retired</u> from <u>farming; and,</u> although he likes to putter in the <u>garden, his</u>
              a   b   c   d

    greatest love is restoration of old furniture. <u>No error.</u>
                                                        e

    a.
    b.
    c.
    d.
    e.

33. <u>Each year,</u> thousands of <u>people consciously decide</u> to vacation in the <u>Far East despite</u> the
          a   b   c

    political <u>turmoil in that</u> part of the world. <u>No error.</u>
                    d   e

    a.
    b.
    c.
    d.
    e.

34. Although <u>David graduated</u> only <u>recently, he</u> acts <u>as if he</u> <u>was running</u> the entire litigation
                      a   b   c   d

    department of the firm. <u>No error.</u>
                                e

    a.
    b.
    c.
    d.
    e.

35. Truman <u>had, by all accounts,</u> established himself as an <u>advocate by</u> making the
                      a   b

    most <u>incredulous legal</u> <u>argument sound like</u> the only reasonable option. <u>No error.</u>
                c   d   e

    a.
    b.
    c.
    d.
    e.

Select the most accurate or most precise definition.

36. baleful
    a. wistful
    b. evil
    c. penitent

37. incongruous
    a. inconsistent
    b. inadvertent
    c. inept

38. canard
    a. species of bird
    b. type of vegetation
    c. false rumor

39. eleemosynary
    a. type of living quarters
    b. pertaining to eels
    c. charitable

40. assiduous
    a. confident
    b. conscientious
    c. stupid

41. assuage
    a. aggravate
    b. accentuate
    c. allay

42. collaborate
    a. combine efforts
    b. verify
    c. build from the ground up

43. enunciate
    a. explain
    b. announce
    c. speak clearly

44. erudite
    a. passive
    b. scholarly
    c. persuasive

45. mundane
    a. ordinary
    b. exceptional
    c. irascible

For each of the following sentences, circle either "a" if the sentence is punctuated correctly or "b" if the sentence is punctuated incorrectly.

46. You may store your books in the attic, but not in the basement.
     a.
     b.

47. The judge was emphatic when he said, that you must comply with the order.
     a.
     b.

48. As hard as I try, I cannot remember the difference between *effect* and *affect*; but I can spell both words correctly.
     a.
     b.

49. The senior partner in our firm is John Doe, but we call him "Black Jack".
     a.
     b.

50. Mary asked, "Where are you going?" when she saw me get up.
     a.
     b.

Fill in each blank with the term or phrase that best fits the definition shown.

51. _____ verbal

52. _____ unique, one of a kind

INTERVIEWING

53. True or False. Initial interviews should be followed by a review of applicable statute and case law.

54. True or False. A witness who knows only a few facts and fills in the gaps with information he believes the interviewer wants to hear is engaged in confabulation.

55. True or False. A telephone interview generates more personal interaction than a personal interview.

56. True or False. Engaging in passive listening during the interview is important to building good rapport.

57. True or False. Slang or jargon used by the witness during an interview should be clarified by the interviewer the moment the term is used rather than waiting until the end of the interview.

58. True or False. Tact is valuable during the interview process, particularly when it comes to discussing uncomfortable events. It is best to avoid the term *rape* when interviewing a client who just experienced a near rape incident.

JUDGMENT AND ANALYTICAL ABILITY

Select the best answer for each of the following questions unless a specific group of questions instructs you to do otherwise.

1. Jane is a paralegal with the firm of Dewey & Billum, where she has worked for the six months since her graduation. Alice Batch, her supervisor, is reputed to have dismissed three employees in the past year for poor performance. Alice, however, also tends to be somewhat brusque in her dealings with clients and staff members alike. In Jane's view, the tasks given to her since her employment (photocopying, running errands, and relaying messages to her clients) could be done by a first-year paralegal student; and she is eager to have more challenging projects. Which of the following options is Jane's best alternative?
   a. Be patient and do nothing.
   b. Try to draft the preliminary prospectus for a public stock offering contemplated in the Simpson case, since Jane knows this must be completed by Friday.
   c. Ask Alice for a project that will allow Jane to use her drafting or organization skills.
   d. Inform Alice's supervisor that Alice is not using Jane's skills effectively.

2. Jack's supervising attorney, Harry, is out of the office for the rest of the week, taking depositions in another city. Jack is very busy, however, summarizing documents in preparation for depositions that will be taken next week. One of the senior partners appears in Jack's office and says, "Since Harry is out of town, I want you to help me by calling potential contributors for the United Way Campaign." Which of the following is the worst response for Jack to give?
   a. "Harry asked me to summarize these documents for next week's depositions; but if you want me to stop now, I will be happy to help with the calls."
   b. "Harry asked me to summarize these documents for next week's depositions, but that can wait."
   c. "Harry asked me to summarize these documents for next week's depositions, but I will be happy to help when I am finished with this project."
   d. "The fact that Harry is out of town does not mean that I have nothing to do."

3. Bill has worked for Mary Lee, a sole practitioner, for several years. While Mary was on the telephone with a client yesterday, Bill heard her say, "I apologize for the error, but Bill must have been confused about which form to use. We will send the correct form right away." Knowing that Mary selected the form herself, Bill was angry about being blamed for her error. What is Bill's best course of action?
   a. Do nothing.
   b. Let Mary know that he heard what she said to the client.
   c. Mention the incident to the legal secretary to prevent the same thing from happening to her.
   d. Call the client and tell him that it was Mary who made the error.

4. The attorney for whom Joe works is extremely unorganized and undisciplined about the way in which he uses his time. It seems to Joe that the lawyer frequently talks on the telephone for days at a time. During those periods, Joe is able to work at an easy pace. Then, without warning, the lawyer decides to attack the paper mountains with a vengeance, and he expects Joe to keep pace with him for two or three days until the lawyer is caught up. Joe, on the other hand, is left with mountains of paper, all with a due date of yesterday. Joe finds this practice unsettling, but he has not been able to motivate the lawyer to use time in a better way. Which of the following represents the best option for Joe?
   a. Find a position in another firm as soon as possible.
   b. Adjust.
   c. Let the attorney know that no reasonable person could work under this type of stress forever.
   d. At the next firm meeting, suggest a workshop or seminar on time management for all of the lawyers.

5. Karen has many years' experience as a paralegal and works for one of the senior partners of a large firm. Part of her job is to help train some of the newer associates. Karen overheard Dan, one of her assigned trainees, say to another young lawyer in the lunchroom, "Well, be glad you don't have to report to that witchy Karen. She's one tough, old broad." When Dan turned in his weekly case report on the following Friday, Karen noticed a number of obvious errors. Before she forwards the report to the senior partner, Karen should
   a. do nothing. (If Dan thinks Karen is tough, wait until he has to deal with the senior partner.)
   b. circle the errors in red and pass the report on to the senior partner, who is certain to chastise Dan.
   c. circle the errors in red and return the report to Dan with a terse memo.
   d. take the report back to Dan and point out the errors, suggesting that his secretary may have misread his handwriting when the report was prepared.

6. Seven is to 21 as _____ is to _____.
   a. 1 : 3
   b. 14 : 28
   c. 8 : 32
   d. 21 : 7

7. Centaur is to horse as _____ is to _____.
   a. woman : mermaid
   b. mermaid : fish
   c. mermaid : woman
   d. fish : mermaid

8. Two is to six as _____ is to _____.
   a. 6 : 2
   b. 3 : 1
   c. 12 : 36
   d. 12 : 60

9. City is to mayor as _____ is to _____.
   a. president : country
   b. government : business
   c. senate : congress
   d. business : manager

10. Pack is to wolves as _____ is to _____.
    a. alphabet : letters
    b. garage : cars
    c. wheel : spokes
    d. aquarium : fish

11. A statute provides that minors "thirteen years of age and under" shall come under the exclusive jurisdiction of the juvenile court except when a case involves murder or treason. Willie Jones stole a car to go joyriding when he was twelve years old, but no charges were filed until he was thirteen years old. Which of the following statements is most correct?
    a. Charges must be filed in juvenile court because Willie is under thirteen years of age.
    b. Charges must be filed in juvenile court because Willie was under thirteen years of age when the offense was committed.
    c. Charges may be filed in adult court because Willie already has passed his thirteenth birthday.
    d. Charges must be filed in adult court because Willie already has passed his thirteenth birthday.

12. Some birds are mammals. Some mammals are carnivorous. Some carnivorous creatures are not birds. Based on these propositions, which of the following could be true?
    a. No mammals are carnivorous.
    b. Some birds are carnivorous.
    c. No carnivorous creatures are mammals.
    d. All mammals are birds.
    e. All birds are carnivorous.

Read this passage and select the best answer to each of the questions that follow it.

Above the west portico of the Supreme Court Building are inscribed the words EQUAL JUSTICE UNDER THE LAW. *At the opposite end of the building, above the east portico, are the words* JUSTICE THE GUARDIAN OF LIBERTY. *These mottos reflect the Court's difficult task: achieving a just balance among the values of freedom, order, and equality. Consider how these values came into conflict in two controversial issues that the Court faced.*

Abortion pits the value of order—the government's responsibility to protect life—against the value of freedom—a woman's right to decide whether or not she will give birth. In the abortion cases beginning with Roe v. Wade, *410 U.S. 113 (1973), the Supreme Court extended the right to privacy to cover a woman's right to terminate a pregnancy. The Court determined that at the beginning of pregnancy, a woman has the right to an abortion, free of government-imposed constraint. However, the Court also recognized that toward the end of pregnancy, government interest in protecting the fetus's right to life generally outweighs a woman's right to abort.*

School desegregation pits the value of equality—equal educational opportunities for minorities—against the value of freedom—the right of parents to send their children to neighborhood schools. In Brown v. Board of Education of Topeka, *347 U.S. 483 (1954), the Supreme Court carried the banner of racial equality by striking down state-mandated segregation in public schools. This decision helped to launch a revolution in race relations in the United States. The justices recognized the disorder their ruling would create but believed that equality clearly outweighed freedom. Twenty-four years later, the Court still was embroiled in controversy over equality when it ruled that race could be a factor in university admissions (to diversify the student body) in the case of* Regents of the University of California v. Bakke, *438 U.S. 265 (1978). In securing equality of blacks, the Court then had to confront the claim that it was denying the freedom of whites.*

The Supreme Court makes national policy. Because its decisions have far-reaching impact, it is vital that we understand how it reaches those decisions. With this understanding, we can better evaluate how the Court fits within our model of democracy.

13. The issue of abortion pits the values of
    a. freedom and order.
    b. freedom and equality.
    c. equality and order.
    d. freedom and racial segregation.

14. The right of parents to send their children to a neighborhood school is
    a. an issue of freedom.
    b. an issue of equality.
    c. denied by the Supreme Court.
    d. denied by the Constitution.

15. True or False. Until forty years ago, it was legal for states to segregate public schools.

16. True or False. The Supreme Court has ruled that universities may use an applicant's race as a consideration in deciding whom they will admit as a student.

17. True or False. In *Roe v. Wade*, the Supreme Court decided that a woman's right to terminate a pregnancy outweighs other rights during the first part of a pregnancy.

Read this passage and select the best answer to each of the questions that follow it.

All Protagonists favored restoration of the monarchy. Some Protagonists favored the maintenance of tyranny if the only alternative was democracy. Any Positivist favoring the maintenance of tyranny did so because he opposed the restoration of a monarchy. All Positivists prefer a democracy.

18. A Protagonist could not adopt which of the following positions?
    a. I favor the maintenance of tyranny over the monarchy.
    b. I favor a monarchy over tyranny.
    c. I favor democracy over tyranny.
    d. If the monarchy cannot be restored, I favor tyranny.
    e. If democracy is the only other alternative, I favor the monarchy.

19. Which of the following positions would a Positivist be most likely to adopt?
    a. I favor tyranny because monarchy is better than democracy.
    b. I am in favor of tyranny.
    c. I am opposed to the monarchy unless it is to avoid democracy.
    d. I am opposed to tyranny unless it is to avoid the monarchy.
    e. I agree with the Protagonists who favor tyranny.

Read this passage and select the best answer to each of the questions that follow it.

I favor the legalization of marijuana. Most arguments favoring such a change focus attention on the dearth of evidence concerning harmful effects of the drug. The effect of such contentions is to neutralize the negative impact of arguments supporting prohibition because of a supposed correlation between the use of marijuana and antisocial behaviors such as murder and rape. Thus far, the burden of constructive argumentation has been borne by the doctrine of individual rights. "Liberty" has been the rallying cry of those who favor legalization. No serious proponent of legislative change has advanced the obvious proposition that marijuana has the beneficial effect of improving human condition by allowing its user to "get high." It is a sad commentary on our culture that pleasure is not recognized as a desideratum but must be justified by some more ponderous purpose.

20. Which of the following statements best reflects the sentiments of the author?
    a. A written constitution is essential to the proper function of the state.
    b. The government should enact stronger consumer protection legislation.
    c. There should be fewer laws restricting individuals.
    d. The government should support more extensive recreation facilities.
    e. All drug laws should be repealed.

21. Which of the following statements would the author believe most weakens his argument?
    a. Marijuana is expensive when compared to alcohol.
    b. Marijuana users frequently experience extreme anxiety.
    c. True human fulfillment is best found in pain and suffering.
    d. Marijuana is highly addictive.
    e. Many people have tried marijuana.

Select the best answer for each of the following questions unless a specific group of questions instructs you to do otherwise.

22. Any radiator without antifreeze will freeze if the temperature dips below 32°F. All radiators will freeze if the temperature drops below 0°F, but no radiator will freeze unless the temperature drops below 32°F. If these statements are true, which of the following conclusions must be false?
    a. Some radiators will freeze at 10 degrees below 0°F.
    b. All radiators may freeze if the temperature falls below 32°F.
    c. No radiator will freeze if the temperature drops below 32°F.
    d. A radiator with antifreeze will not freeze if the temperature drops below 0°F.
    e. All radiators will not freeze if the temperature remains above 32°F.

23. True or False. The exercise of good judgment requires an understanding of the chain of command within a law firm as well as familiarity with the idiosyncrasies of those who supervise the paralegal.

24. True or False. A paralegal reasonably may assume that if his or her conduct falls within the parameters of the law and of current ethics rules, he or she may engage in that conduct without encountering problems.

25. True or False. If the office policies and procedures manual dictates a particular procedure, but your supervising attorney insists on a different procedure, your best course of action is to follow the office manual.

26. True or False. Sam is a paralegal at Dewey & Billum. In a depressed economy, the firm has been downsizing for several months. At yesterday's firm meeting, the legal administrator announced that until the situation becomes more stable, everyone on the staff must work every other Saturday morning. Sam never has worked on Saturdays and values his weekends, when family events occur. Sam's best alternative is to cooperate with the Saturday mandate, at least for now.

27. Although alcohol seems to make a person sleepy, it is an anti-sopoforic. The logic of this statement is most closely paralleled by the logic of which of the following?
    a. Although some people still believe in God, many people have accepted science as supreme.
    b. Although sea water will not quench thirst, it will extinguish fires.
    c. Although dry ice seems to burn the skin of those who touch it, it is quite cold.
    d. All states have a capital. Providence is the capital of Rhode Island. Therefore, Rhode Island is a state.

28. According to the tenor of the following statements and the apparent authority of the source, which of the following is most reliable?
    a. Aide to Senator: "Senator Allen's aide told me that his senator would support your bill."
    b. Student to Teacher: "I cannot give you the assignment that is due today because my dog chewed it to pieces."
    c. Mayor to Reporter: "I cannot remember how much income tax I paid last year."
    d. Preacher to Congregation: "There can be no doubt that God exists."

29. A cryptographer intercepted an enemy message that is in code. He knows that the code is a simple substitution of numbers for letters. Which of the following will be least helpful in breaking the code?
    a. Knowing the frequency with which the vowels of the language are used.
    b. Knowing the frequency with which two vowels appear together in the language.
    c. Knowing the frequency with which odd numbers appear relative to even numbers in the message.
    d. Knowing every word in the language that begins with the letter *r*.

30. A television advertisement stated, "For fast, fast, fast relief of pain, take Slammer. Per dose, Slammer has twice as much of the pain reliever most recommended by doctors as any other brand of product." Which of the following most weakens the argument of the advertisement?
    a. The pain reliever contained in Slammer is simple aspirin.
    b. Most doctors do not recommend Slammer.
    c. The body can absorb only one-fourth of the pain reliever contained in Slammer.
    d. Slammer costs twice as much as any other brand.

31. The protection of property rights by the Constitution is tenuous at best. It is true that the Fifth Amendment states that a government may not take private property for public use without compensation, but it is the government that defines private property. It may be inferred that the author also believes which of the following?
    a. Individual rights protected by the Supreme Court are secure against government infringement.
    b. Private property is neither more nor less than that which the government says is private property.
    c. The government has no authority to deprive an individual of his or her liberty.
    d. No government that acts arbitrarily can be justified.

32. Which of the following statements most weakens the author's argument in the immediately preceding question?
    a. The government has mandated that employers cannot fire employees for union activity.
    b. The government has placed a tax on both corporate and individual income.
    c. The power to take private property is vested in the executive branch, while the authority to define private property and to award compensation is vested in the judicial branch.
    d. Only a handful of people actually own property.

33. "When did you stop beating your wife?" The form of this question most closely parallels which of the following?
    a. Do you believe that children should support their parents?
    b. If I let you go this time, will you promise never to do that again?
    c. When is the best time for planting corn?
    d. When did Caesar cross the Rubicon?

34. "All red rosebushes have thorns. This bush has no thorns. Therefore, this cannot be a rosebush." The logic of this thought pattern most closely parallels which of the following?
    a. All Suzu automobiles have three wheels. This car has three wheels. Therefore, it is a Suzu automobile.
    b. All virgin brides wear white. This woman is not wearing white. Therefore, she must be the best man.
    c. All Scottish ivy is heliotropic. This plant is not heliotropic. Therefore, it cannot be ivy.
    d. All pencils have rubber erasers. This eraser is not on a pencil. Therefore, it cannot be rubber.

35. "The whole is equal to the sum of its parts." The logic of this statement is paralleled by all but which of the following statements?
    a. Mass can be neither created nor destroyed, but only altered in appearance.
    b. Community values are the sum of the values held by the individuals in the community.
    c. A family unit is something more than simply parents and children living together.
    d. Anything with four legs, a back, and a seat is a chair.

36. "All judgments regarding values such as truth, beauty, and justice inherently are a matter of individual choice and are, therefore, subjective. They carry no moral authority for any but the individual who selects them." Of the following attacks on the author's argument, which is the strongest?
    a. Holy scripture tells us that there are such absolute values.
    b. Plato stated that there are values that have meaning for all men at all times.
    c. If the statement is true, it carries moral force only for the person formulating it and it does not apply to others.
    d. There is no need to arrive at content for such concepts.

37. Sir Sidney Wacker was lost deep in the darkest reaches of Kansas. While walking along the Yellow Brick Road, which he hoped eventually would return him to the Industrial Diamond City, he encountered a fork. He knew that one road must take him to the city; the other, to the castle of the wicked witch of Topeka. He saw a farmer standing in a nearby cornfield. Sir Sidney knew there were two types of farmers in this region, those who always told the truth and those that always told the opposite of the truth. Sir Sidney knew he had time to ask only one question of the farmer, for an ominous dark cloud was about to overtake him. Which of the following questions would have ensured Sir Sidney's finding the right road?
    a. If I asked you if this is the road to town, would you say yes?
    b. If I asked you if this is the road to town, would you tell the truth?
    c. Which is the road to town?
    d. Is this not the road that does not lead to town?

38. Maguire decided he would have a portrait of himself painted by an internationally renowned artist, L'Artiste. He paid L'Artiste $25,000 and posed several times. When the painting was delivered three months later, it was signed not by L'Artiste but by Le Peintre, an equally famous artist. L'Artiste explained that he had been too busy and had asked Le Peintre to take over some of his work. Maguire sued L'Artiste, and the court held for Maguire. Which of the following principles explains the result most narrowly?
    a. A party to a contract legally is entitled to insist upon performance of the obligations by the promisor.
    b. Where the performance of the contract materially would be altered, a promisor may not delegate another to perform his obligations.
    c. In a contract for personal service, the promisee may reject the promisor's performance if he deems it improper or unsatisfactory.
    d. A promisor to a contract is under a duty to perform personally all of the services required of him by the contract.

39. Gay sold an automobile to Maura for $3,000 in 1990, and Maura signed a promissory note that called for payment of $3,500 in 1993. Following this transaction, the two had an argument. Gay anxiously awaited the due date for the loan. Knowing that Maura could not pay the note, Gay hoped to embarrass her by filing a lawsuit. On the due date, Maura's sister came to Gay with $3,500 and announced that she had come to repay the loan. Gay refused to accept the money and sued Maura. The court held for Maura. Which of the following principles most narrowly explains this result and is not inconsistent with the ruling in the previous case?
    a. A promisee has no legal right to insist that performance under a contract be made directly by the promisor.
    b. The debtor in a debtor-creditor relationship may appoint another to pay the debt to a third party, and the third party must substitute that person for the promisor.
    c. A promisee must accept the performance of a contractual obligation if it is offered by a close relative.
    d. Where reasonable satisfaction of the contractual obligation has been offered, the promisee is required to accept that satisfaction in discharge of the promised performance.

40. Dick owned a piece of land, Blackacre, which he advertised for sale at $3,000. Tom signed a contract with Dick that stated, "Next Wednesday, Dick will convey Blackacre to Tom in exchange for $3,000." On Tuesday, Potts Oil Company announced that there was likely a large pool of oil beneath Blackacre. Dick refused to go through with the deal. Tom sued Dick to force the sale, and the court held for Tom. Which of the following principles most narrowly explains this ruling and is not inconsistent with the rulings given in the previous two cases?

   a. Where the subject matter of the contract is unique, a court may order the promisor to perform if such an order is administratively practical.
   b. A written contract for the sale of land is final and binding on the parties.
   c. A court may order specific enforcement of a contract where the promisor refuses to honor his side of the bargain.
   d. The promisee has a legal right to insist upon the exact performance promised by the promisor.

ETHICS

Select the best answer for each of the following questions unless a specific group of questions instructs you to do otherwise.

1. Jane is a rehabilitation nurse working with individuals who have been injured on the job. Her brother and sister recently graduated from law school and opened their own firm specializing in workers' compensation and personal injury. Looking for sources of referral, the lawyers propose to Jane that for every patient referred to them, they will pay Jane ten percent of any fee collected as a "finder's fee." Which of the following is most accurate?
   a. This is permissible because Jane is not part of the law firm.
   b. This is an acceptable practice because the lawyers have a financial obligation to the client to represent the client zealously; thus, the lawyer is motivated to seek the largest recovery for the client.
   c. The lawyers cannot fee-split with nonlawyers.
   d. If Jane had been employed by the law firm as a nurse-paralegal, splitting the fee would be acceptable.

2. True or False. Fees may be split between lawyers associated with separate offices if the client consents to the employment of both attorneys and to the percentage of fees to each, provided the fee is not excessive.

3. Attorney Timmy Testosterone is a handsome bachelor in Papillion who has a reputation as an excellent divorce lawyer. His client, Dave Dudd, suggests that Timmy obtain whatever particulars possible from Dottie Dudd, Dave's soon-to-be ex-wife. Dave makes it known that he wants custody of the children. Dave casually mentions to Timmy that Dottie uses cocaine. Timmy contacts a friend at the police department to obtain some confiscated cocaine. Soon after, Timmy visits Dottie, who enjoys the cocaine and Timmy's company. During the evening, Dottie discloses information that is damaging to her credibility as a parent. Timmy tucks away this new information in the event he needs to use it. After leaving Dottie, Timmy informs his detective friend of the whereabouts of Dottie's cocaine and she is arrested for possession. Dave is delighted because he is sure this will aid him in getting custody of the children. What are the ethical concerns?
   a. Timmy Testosterone engaged in activities that are analogous with overly zealous representation.
   b. Timmy Testosterone engaged in illegal activity to secure damaging information for his own client.
   c. It is the lawyer's responsibility to reveal to the court that Dottie Dudd is an illegal drug user.
   d. a and b

4. A lawyer may accept ownership interest in a business for payment of services but cannot accept a proprietary interest in the outcome of a case. This type of proprietary interest is forbidden and is referred to as
   a. assumpsit.
   b. compos mentis.
   c. champerty.
   d. pro hac vice.

5. Larry Paralegal and his supervising lawyer are involved in a real estate development transaction for a client for building a multilevel shopping and business center. The area to be developed is in a blighted area of the city. This development will result in dramatic increases in property values in the surrounding areas. Three weeks after the transaction is completed, Larry and his employer-lawyer, along with friends, purchase real estate surrounding the potential business center. Any ethical problems?
   a. Yes, it is prohibited for lawyers and nonlawyers to engage in a business enterprise together.
   b. No problems exist.
   c. To avoid the appearance of impropriety, more time should have elapsed from the completion date of the transaction to the date of purchase.
   d. Yes, disclosure of confidential information was used inappropriately for personal gain.

6. Disclosing one's status as a paralegal is important because
   a. the nonlawyer is engaging in the unauthorized practice of law if he or she appears to others to be an attorney.
   b. the client may ask for legal advice if he or she believes the paralegal is a lawyer.
   c. it eliminates confusion by the client of the role of the nonlawyer.
   d. all of the above
   e. none of the above

7. Which of the following typically is not held in a client trust fund?
   a. estate or trust distributions
   b. real estate closing distributions
   c. a retainer
   d. PAC fund distributions

8. True or False. If a client is a business client, such as a partnership or corporation, names of its subsidiaries, shareholders, directors, officers, and partners should be revealed for a conflict check.

9. True or False. Two reasons for the doctrine of unauthorized practice of law are to prevent the unscrupulous from taking advantage of the public and to protect the public against uninsured legal practitioners.

10. True or False. The attorney-client privilege ends when the representation ends, but anything learned during representation from that point need not be protected by the attorney or paralegal.

11. The doctrine that covers the elements of work produced by the attorney or by any of his or her agents and that precludes the disclosure of any such work during representation is known as
    a. the code of silence.
    b. the work product.
    c. confidentiality.
    d. representation.

12. A reprimand issued to an attorney for an ethical violation may be given
    a. publicly.
    b. in open court before other members of the bar.
    c. privately in the judge's or bar official's chambers.
    d. all of the above
    e. none of the above

13. Paul and Cherrie Blossum, brother and sister, rent a condominium from Terry Tempest. Paul is a high school dropout. He loses his job and falls behind on the rent payments for five months. Terry Tempest files a dispossessory action against Paul and Cherrie. Cherrie accepts the sheriff's service for herself and for her brother. At the hearing, Cherrie appears without Paul, gives the judge a document signed by Paul granting Cherrie the authority to represent him, and informs the judge she is there to argue the matter for both of them. Any ethical problems?
    a. Yes, a nonlawyer cannot argue questions of law.
    b. No, Paul has given Cherrie written permission to represent him since he is not skilled to present his own argument.
    c. Yes, Cherrie cannot represent anyone but herself before a court of law.
    d. No, matters of landlord-tenant are decided before an administrative agency, which means nonlawyers can represent themselves and others.

14. True or False. A Chinese Wall is also known as a code of silence.

15. True or False. It is permissible for a lawyer to draft a document, such as a will or a trust, under which he or she will receive a gift.

16. True or False. The ABA Model Rules of Professional Conduct prohibit an attorney from entering into an agreement granting the attorney publication, literary, or media rights pertaining to a current case before the conclusion of that representation.

17. A long-standing client of the firm calls the paralegal, informing him that the supervising lawyer had agreed to prepare a will for her. However, during their conversation, the client forgot to ask the amount of the fee for preparing the will. The client asks the paralegal. How should the paralegal respond?
    a. "The last will prepared by Attorney Beaton cost the client $125. Your situation is similar, so the fee should be about the same."
    b. "The firm's fee schedule indicates that simple wills are $100."
    c. "Attorney Beaton will return your call after lunch to quote you a fee."
    d. "Being a paralegal, I am prohibited by law from discussing the fee with you. Let me ask Attorney Beaton to return your call."

18. A paralegal moves from one law firm to another. A conflict-of-interest check is made after employment is offered to the paralegal but before the paralegal moves to the new firm. The new firm discovers a conflict with the firm where the paralegal is employed. What is the best approach to address this dilemma?
    a. The new law firm should withdraw its offer of employment.
    b. The new law firm should contact the supervising attorney of the paralegal after obtaining permission from the paralegal, inform the attorney of the offer of employment to the paralegal, and propose a plan for isolating the paralegal from the case at the new firm.
    c. Discuss the implications with the paralegal and establish a Chinese Wall at the new firm.
    d. The new law firm should explain to the paralegal that he or she will not be working on any existing files but will have responsibility only for new matters.

19. Which of the following is not a proper guideline for avoiding improprieties regarding the issue of zealous representation?
    a. Do not discuss anything with an opposing party, other than to notify him or her of the need for representation.
    b. Do not talk with a juror except in limited circumstances after completion of trial.
    c. Meet frequently with the judge during a trial so that he or she is fully informed of the facts of the matter.
    d. Avoid talking to the media during a case.

20. True or False. If a client pays a retainer to a lawyer, the lawyer cannot remove any of the funds, except for advanced costs, from the client trust account until the case is complete.

21. True or False. Lawyers may send advertising material to individuals, provided the envelope clearly states "This is advertising material."

22. Pro bono work
    a. is legal work that legal professionals offer free of charge.
    b. helps create a positive image of the legal profession.
    c. allows legal professionals to "give back" to the community.
    d. a and c
    e. all of the above

23. The NALA Model Standards and Guidelines for the Utilization of Paralegals contains
    a. a definition of a paralegal.
    b. education criteria for a paralegal.
    c. utilization criteria for a paralegal.
    d. a and c
    e. all of the above
    f. none of the above

24. Joe Jokk sues Harry Kerry for default on a promissory note. Harry Kerry employs Attorney Betty Beatus. Near the end of the litigation on this matter, Joe Jokk asks Attorney Beatus to handle a traffic violation for him. Can Attorney Beatus represent both Mr. Jokk and Mr. Kerry at the same time?
    a. No, the ABA Model Rules of Professional Conduct explicitly prohibit an attorney from dual representation.
    b. Yes, as long as the attorney fully discloses the dual representation to both Mr. Kerry and Mr. Jokk.
    c. Yes, however, the attorney needs to fully disclose to Mr. Kerry this potential conflict of interest and obtain his consent, preferably in writing, before accepting the traffic violation matter. Also, Mr. Jokk's consent needs to be obtained, preferably in writing.
    d. Yes, but permission for the dual representation needs to be obtained from Mr. Kerry, Mr. Jokk, and Mr. Jokk's attorney in the promissory note action.

25. True or False. Attorney Axel represents a corporation. During an interview, a corporate employee discloses information damaging to himself personally but advantageous to the corporation. Attorney Axel's duty of confidentiality is to the corporate employee as an agent of the corporation.

26. John Deever is divorcing Patty. John has attempted to visit Patty numerous times during the divorce action. Several times Patty has been with a group of friends when John arrives. Each time John comes to Patty's home, the same gentleman friend is among the group visiting with Patty, and John begins to suspect that Patty is having an affair with this gentleman. Patty refuses to let John inside her home, which makes John very angry. Each visit results in a more intense argument between Patty and John. John appears uncontrollably angry and bitter after his last visit at Patty's. That afternoon, John storms into his attorney's office and sees Lela Paralegal. The attorney is out of the city and left no forwarding telephone number. (The law office has only one attorney and one paralegal.) John is enraged and makes the following statement, "I'm going to take care of her tonight once and for all." Lela never has seen John this angry. What should Lela do?
    a. Call a good attorney friend, explain the situation, and seek advice.
    b. Ignore John because he is a hothead and will cool down on his own.
    c. Call the judge in the matter and seek her advice.
    d. Call the proper authorities (i.e., police, sheriff) and inform them of the threat.
    e. none of the above

27. True or False. Using the preceding example, the paralegal can do nothing because the communication provided by John to the law office is confidential.

28. True or False. If a client files a malpractice claim against his or her attorney, the attorney may use confidential communication gained while representing that client to defend the malpractice claim.

29. True or False. It is permissible for a paralegal to negotiate a settlement up to a certain reasonable amount if authorized by an attorney.

30. Rosemary opened a secretarial service to help her clients prepare pleadings so they could represent themselves. Rosemary had the clients prepare an information sheet, but sometimes the information was incomplete because the clients were unsure how to complete the document. Rosemary contacted the clients to obtain the information and completed the form herself. She further provided direction to the clients about how to represent themselves in court. Rosemary's charge was $50. Were Rosemary's services permissible under the ABA Model Rules of Professional Conduct?
    a. Yes. Rosemary did not represent the client in court; she only provided direction outside the courtroom.
    b. No. Rosemary engaged in the practice of law because she advised, assisted, and communicated with the clients regarding the pleadings.
    c. Yes. Rosemary provided only a typing service.
    d. No. Rosemary is not permitted to charge for these services.

31. True or False. A paralegal may appear on behalf of a client before the National Labor Relations Board.

32. True or False. During a witness interview, the witness provides convincing information to Lulu Legal Assistant indicating her firm's client may have intentionally run over his former business partner. If Lulu is later deposed concerning this interview, she could refuse to answer questions based on confidentiality principles.

33. True or False. Under the ABA Model Rules of Professional Conduct, there is a precise definition for the "practice of law."

34. True or False. The fee arrangement between a lawyer and a client is privileged information.

35. Although the lawyer is responsible for making decisions concerning legal strategies, the client must be included in the decision-making process concerning
    a. acceptance of a settlement.
    b. incurring extraordinary expenses.
    c. third parties who may be adversely affected.
    d. a and b
    e. all of the above
    f. none of the above

36. Contingency fees are prohibited in cases involving
    a. divorce.
    b. personal injury.
    c. criminal charges.
    d. a and c
    e. none of the above

37. True or False. Learning the client is guilty after the criminal action has been initiated is a valid basis for withdrawing representation.

38. True or False. A longtime client calls the paralegal and asks the paralegal's personal opinion regarding withdrawal of money from a joint account in view of a temporary restraining order that was just entered. The client realizes the paralegal is not a lawyer, but the client would like to know what the paralegal would do under these circumstances. Since it is only personal opinion and not legal advice, it is permissible for the paralegal to answer.

39. The attorney promised certain documents would be mailed to the client by a particular date. The documents are on the attorney's desk, but she has not reviewed them. The client insists the documents be mailed at once; otherwise, he will find an attorney who can produce the work. The attorney practices alone and cannot be reached for the rest of the day. What is the best alternative for the paralegal?
    a. Politely refuse to send the documents.
    b. Send the documents but stamp "Draft Documents, For Discussion Only" and send a cover letter indicating these are drafts that have not been reviewed by the attorney.
    c. Be polite and indicate the documents will be mailed soon. In the meantime, leave a message at the attorney's hotel to call immediately. With the permission of the attorney, deliver or fax the documents to the client the next day.
    d. Wait until the attorney returns to the office so she can review the drafts and then send the documents.

40. True or False. It is proper to bill the client for paralegal time in collating and photocopying trial exhibits.

41. True or False. Office politics should be avoided.

42. True or False. To seek further clarification during a witness interview, it is permissible to misstate information provided by the witness in order to generate more narrative.

43. True or False. When the client criticizes the opposing party or opposing attorney, the paralegal should remain neutral concerning such statements.

44. True or False. Probing the client or the witness during an interview is unprofessional and should be avoided.

45. True or False. If a witness is deliberately lying during an interview, the paralegal should confront the witness with the misstatements and ask the witness to leave.

46. True or False. During the investigative and trial preparation periods, the paralegal should maintain a businesslike, professional relationship with the client; there should be minimal discussion with the client concerning his or her family.

47. True or False. At a field interview, the paralegal should present his or her business card to the witness.

48. True or False. During a taped telephone interview, the interviewer should remind the witness different times during the interview that the conversation is being taped.

LEGAL RESEARCH

Select the best answer for each of the following questions unless a specific group of questions instructs you to do otherwise.

1. True or False. A.L.R. is part of West's American Digest System.

2. True or False. C.J.S. uses the West key number system.

3. True or False. Statutes are published as slip laws before they are published as session laws.

4. True or False. Statutes are published as session laws at the close of each legislative term.

5. True or False. *Statutes at Large* is an official publication and includes all laws enacted by Congress.

6. True or False. The *Federal Supplement* is an official case reporter.

7. True or False. The *Federal Supplement* contains only selected decisions of federal district courts across the country.

8. True or False. Annotations and summarized briefs of counsel are hallmarks of the Supreme Court Reports.

9. True or False. A researcher should cite to the most recent digest where a particular case summary is found.

10. True or False. *Murray on Contracts* is a treatise.

11. Case law concerning federal rules of procedure is collected in
    a. *U.S. Law Week.*
    b. *Federal Rules Decisions.*
    c. *United States Code.*
    d. *American Law Reports.*

12. The official publication for congressional session laws is
    a. *United States Code.*
    b. *United States Reports.*
    c. *Federal Reporter, Second Series.*
    d. *Statutes at Large.*

13. An annotation is a(n)
    a. explanatory note.
    b. brief summary of a case.
    c. brief summary of the holding of a case.
    d. detailed summary of a rule of law.

14. A Decennial Digest is part of the
    a. West Reporter System.
    b. American Digest System.
    c. American Law System.
    d. Regional Reporter System.

15. The cases reported in *Federal Reporter, Second Series,* include
    a. all cases decided by federal courts of appeals.
    b. cases from federal courts of appeals, as selected by West editors.
    c. cases from federal courts of appeals, as selected by the judges.
    d. cases from federal courts of appeals, as ordered by the judges.

16. When a judge disagrees with both the reasoning and result of the majority, but also disagrees with the dissenting opinion, he or she may write
    a. a concurring opinion.
    b. a per curiam opinion.
    c. a second dissenting opinion.
    d. no opinion.

17. Before 1924, cases from the U.S. Court of Appeals and the U.S. District Court were combined in
    a. *Federal Cases.*
    b. the *Federal Reporter.*
    c. the *Federal Supplement.*
    d. the *Federal Reporter, Second Series.*

18. Star paging is contained in
    a. the first 90 volumes of *U.S. Reports.*
    b. *Supreme Court Reporter.*
    c. *Supreme Court Reporter, Lawyers Edition.*
    d. all of the above
    e. two of the above

19. *American Jurisprudence* is a(n)
    a. treatise.
    b. digest.
    c. encyclopedia.
    d. case reporter.

20. *U.S. Law Week*
    a. contains recent decisions of the U.S. Supreme Court.
    b. contains recent decisions of all federal appellate courts.
    c. is an official publication.
    d. all of the above

21. True or False. The *Federal Register* is an official publication.

22. True or False. *Supreme Court Reports* is an official publication.

23. True or False. The *Federal Supplement* is an official publication.

24. True or False. *United States Reports* is an official publication.

25. True or False. The *Code of Federal Regulations* is an official publication.

26. True or False. The *United States Code Service* is an official publication.

27. True or False. The *Atlantic Reporter, Second Series,* is an official publication.

28. True or False. The *United States Code* is an official publication.

29. True or False. The *Supreme Court Reporter, Lawyers Edition,* is an official publication.

30. True or False. The *Federal Reporter, Second Edition,* is an official publication.

31. The primary finding tool for case law, either state or federal, is a(n)
    a. digest.
    b. index.
    c. *Shepard's.*
    d. encyclopedia.

32. The primary finding tool for statutory law, either state or federal, is
    a. a digest.
    b. an index.
    c. *Shepard's.*
    d. an encyclopedia.

33. If a researcher wants to check the current status of a case, he or she should use
    a. a supplement.
    b. *Shepard's* Citations.
    c. a digest.
    d. two of the above
    e. all of the above

34. If a researcher wants to check the current status of a statute, he or she should use
    a. a supplement.
    b. *Shepard's* Citations.
    c. a digest.
    d. two of the above
    e. all of the above

35. *U.S. Reports* contains
    a. a syllabus of the court.
    b. headnotes of editors.
    c. summaries of briefs of counsel.
    d. references to other sources.
    e. all of the above

36. A scope note tells a researcher coverage of a particular
    a. index topic.
    b. encyclopedia topic.
    c. digest topic.
    d. A.L.R. topic.

37. A.L.R. is
    a. filled with key number references.
    b. filled with extensive selected annotations.
    c. an official publication.
    d. an encyclopedia.

38. Executive orders are
    a. secondary law.
    b. statutory law.
    c. procedural law.
    d. all of the above

39. Federal rules and regulations are
    a. secondary law.
    b. statutory law.
    c. procedural law.
    d. all of the above

40. An unofficial publication is any publication
    a. of primary law authorized and issued by Congress.
    b. of primary law authorized and issued by the Supreme Court.
    c. (primary law, secondary law, encyclopedia, or other) issued by a private, nongovernment publisher.
    d. that the Supreme Court or Congress has disapproved specifically.

41. Nearly every reporter contains
    a. a descriptive word index.
    b. a subsequent history of each case reported.
    c. research topics and accompanying key numbers.
    d. all of the above

42. Which of the following represent secondary authority?
    a. treatise, Supreme Court case, law review article, executive order
    b. digest, index, encyclopedia, treatise
    c. restatement of law, encyclopedia, law review article, treatise
    d. encyclopedia, legal dictionary, treatise, slip law

43. Which of the following represent primary authority?
    a. rules of procedure, local court rules, executive orders, administrative regulations
    b. common law, session laws, executive orders, annotations
    c. case law from equal or lower jurisdiction, statutes, Constitution, common law
    d. common law, statutes, Constitution, treatise

44. True or False. The National Reporter System and the American Digest System are products of West Legal Studies.

45. True or False. The National Reporter System divides the country into seven regions.

46. True or False. A statutory code is arranged by statute number.

47. True or False. To determine whether a particular Nebraska case was reversed in the U.S. Supreme Court, a researcher should consult *Shepard's* Nebraska Citations.

48. Which of the following is (are) shown in correct citation form?
    a. *Ace v. Deuce*, 453 U.S. 766 (1993)
    b. *Ace v. Deuce*, 453 U.S. 766, 497 S. Ct. 109, 613 L. Ed .2d 345 (1993)
    c. *Ace v. Deuce*, 644 F.2d 987 (4th Cir. 1993)
    d. two of the above
    e. all of the above
    f. none of the above

49. Which of the following is (are) not shown in the correct citation form?
    a. *Ace v. Deuce R.R. Co.*, 453 U.S. 766 (1993)
    b. *Ace v. Deuce*, 766 F. Supp. 613 (D. Neb. 1993)
    c. 19 C.J.S. *Constitutional Law* § 256, 261 (1989)
    d. two of the above
    e. all of the above
    f. none of the above

50. Which of the following is (are) shown in the correct citation form?
    a. *Burton v. Smith*, 467 F. Supp. 922 (E. D. Pa. 1993)
    b. *Id.* at 924
    c. *Burton*, 467 F. Supp. at 925
    d. two of the above
    e. all of the above
    f. none of the above

Fill in the blank with the term or phrase that best fits the definition below.

51. _____ among other things

52. _____ notwithstanding

53. _____ illogical, does not follow

54. _____ Latin term meaning "note well"

SUBSTANTIVE LAW

(includes General Law—American Legal System, Business Organizations, Contracts and Civil Litigation)

GENERAL LAW—AMERICAN LEGAL SYSTEM

Select the best answer for each of the following questions unless a specific group of questions instructs you to do otherwise.

1. True or False. The federal bankruptcy court is an Article III court.

2. True or False. Judges of the federal district court are appointed by the president, with approval by the Senate.

3. True or False. Only the U.S. District Court has jurisdiction to hear cases involving foreign ambassadors.

4. True or False. A *Miranda* warning is required because of the protections of the Fifth Amendment.

5. True or False. Most uniform laws originated from the National Conference of Commissioners on Uniform State Laws.

6. True or False. Civil law has existed since before the time of Christ.

7. True or False. Common law has existed since before the time of Christ.

8. True or False. One who seeks a patent may do so under federal law and under the state law of most states.

9. True or False. The U.S. Supreme Court is the supreme law of the land.

10. True or False. If it chose to do so, Congress could eliminate the U.S. Court of Appeals.

11. Executive orders adopted by the president are classified as
    a. common law.
    b. statutory law.
    c. administrative law.
    d. procedural law.

12. Which of the following is (are) classified as primary law?
    a. federal rules of procedure
    b. administrative rules and regulations
    c. executive orders
    d. local court rules
    e. two of the above
    f. all of the above

13. The U.S. Supreme Court may hear appellate cases by
    a. writ of certiorari.
    b. appeal of right.
    c. writ of mandamus.
    d. two of the above
    e. all of the above

14. Treaties between the United States and foreign nations are signed by the president and ratified by
    a. the House of Representatives.
    b. the Senate.
    c. both houses of Congress.
    d. no ratification is necessary.

15. The term used to signify that federal authority is allocated among the legislative, executive, and judicial branches of government is
    a. separation of powers.
    b. federalism.
    c. preemption.
    d. supremacy.

16. As a minimum, procedural due process requires
    a. procedural rules that are fundamentally fair.
    b. a fair hearing.
    c. notice and an opportunity to be heard.
    d. rules that are neither arbitrary nor capricious.

17. Juries decide
    a. law.
    b. facts.
    c. law and facts in simple cases.
    d. all of the above

18. A capital crime is one
    a. punishable by death or imprisonment.
    b. against the federal government.
    c. committed in the nation's capital.
    d. punishable by imprisonment of more than one year.

19. If Kentucky wishes to file suit against Tennessee for violation of an interstate compact, the suit may be filed in the
    a. U.S. Supreme Court.
    b. U.S. District Court.
    c. state court of either Kentucky or Tennessee.
    d. any one or more of the above

20. Decisions of administrative agencies must be supported by
    a. proof beyond a reasonable doubt.
    b. a preponderance of evidence.
    c. clear and convincing evidence.
    d. substantial evidence.

21. True or False. Habeas corpus refers to a post-conviction criminal proceeding.

22. True or False. A maxim of equity courts is that "one who comes into equity must come with a clean heart."

23. True or False. Rules adopted by administrative agencies are classified as statutory law.

24. True or False. The federal government is a government of limited powers.

25. True or False. The doctrine that requires like cases to be decided in the same way is called stare decisis.

26. True or False. There are eleven regions or circuits in the federal judicial system.

27. True or False. The legal doctrine that prevents the same issues from being relitigated between the same parties is res gestae.

28. True or False. One who creates new types of vegetation may protect his or her creations under federal patent laws.

29. True or False. Justices of the U.S. Supreme Court are nominated by the House of Representatives, with approval by the Senate.

30. True or False. A person who commits murder may be prosecuted either in federal court or in state court.

31. Diversity jurisdiction in federal district court requires
    a. citizens from different states and an amount in controversy of $75,000.
    b. citizens from different states and an amount in controversy of more than $75,000.
    c. citizens from different states and an amount in controversy of not less than $75,000.
    d. none of the above

32. A jury of twelve peers in civil cases is
    a. required by the Supremacy Clause of the Constitution.
    b. required by the Sixth Amendment of the Constitution.
    c. required by Article III of the Constitution.
    d. not required by the Constitution.

33. The right of privacy is protected by the
    a. First Amendment of the Constitution.
    b. Fifth Amendment of the Constitution.
    c. Sixth Amendment of the Constitution.
    d. none of the above

34. A distinguishing feature of equity courts is that
    a. they are established by specific statute.
    b. they have contempt powers.
    c. no jury trials are allowed.
    d. their decisions are not subject to appeal.

35. The predecessor of today's equity courts was the
    a. Court of Common Pleas.
    b. King's Court.
    c. Roman Court of Equity.
    d. Chancery Court.

36. True or False. The principle of stare decisis prevents a court from deviating from rules of precedent set in prior cases.

37. True or False. The term *original jurisdiction* is used to signify that more than one court has the power to conduct a trial of a particular case and to render a decision on the merits.

38. True or False. If a court enters an order sua sponte, the court enters the order on its own motion rather than on the motion of counsel.

39. The science or system of law is called
    a. jurisprudence.
    b. jurisdiction.
    c. jus tertii.
    d. lex nexus.

40. The power of a court to hear a particular matter and to render a decision on the merits is determined by the court's
    a. jurisprudence.
    b. jurisdiction.
    c. judicature.
    d. adjudication.

For the next group of questions, fill in each blank with the term or phrase that best fits the definition shown.

41. _____ notice of suit issued by the court to a defendant

42. _____ false testimony given under oath

43. _____ application to a court that is not a pleading

BUSINESS ORGANIZATIONS

Select the best answer for each of the following questions unless a specific group of questions instructs you to do otherwise.

1. True or False. Stock issued for less than par value is known as watered stock.

2. Jack is a delivery driver for Daffy's Taffy, Inc., a corporation. On Friday, May 13, Jack drives his delivery truck into the rear of Fee-Fee LuPue's car. Fee-Fee sustains injuries and is taken by ambulance to the hospital. Fee-Fee remains in the hospital for several days, misses work, and attends therapy for three weeks. Under what theory can Fee-Fee sue Jack's employer for damages?
    a. corporation by estoppel
    b. respondeat superior
    c. de facto
    d. de jure

3. Preemptive rights are exercised
    a. to convert common shares to preferred stock to place the interest of the shareholder in a more favorable holding position.
    b. to give initial investors the opportunity to invest additional monies during the preincorporation stage of the corporation.
    c. by the members of the board of directors who are shareholders to purchase additional shares of stock before offering stock to outsiders.
    d. to protect a shareholder's proportionate interest in the corporation.

4. Redemption of stock is
   a. redeeming voting rights in exchange for receipt of dividends.
   b. giving up the stock in exchange for corporate assets.
   c. classified as corporate leverage.
   d. applied only to nonvoting common stock.

5. True or False. Short-term share options are called stock rights.

6. The persons who plan and organize the business affairs of the intended corporation are called
   a. incorporators.
   b. promoters.
   c. investors.
   d. stockholders.

Choose the worst answer for Questions 7 through 9.

7. A joint venture
   a. involves efforts of two or more persons for one transaction or event only.
   b. resembles a partnership.
   c. has perpetual existence.
   d. may be reduced to writing.

8. Liability of limited partners is limited unless
   a. the limited partner's name is part of the name of the limited partnership.
   b. the limited partner has no management responsibilities.
   c. false statements are in the certificate of partnership.
   d. the limited partner takes no action to correct the defects in the certificate of partnership.

9. The court may order liquidation of a corporation if the suit is initiated by the shareholders and if
   a. the directors are deadlocked over management issues and harm comes to the corporation.
   b. acts by the directors or those in control are oppressive.
   c. corporate assets are being wasted.
   d. the shareholders have elected new directors to correct the problems.

Select the best answer for each of the following questions.

10. True or False. Conflict of interest may arise when an officer of a corporation serves on the board of directors of another corporation.

11. True or False. Self-executing statutes remove a director's liability involving money damage suits.

12. True or False. A stock split decreases the total number of outstanding shares without distributing corporate assets.

13. Offering a shareholder the right to purchase a specific number of shares of a designated class for a limited time at a certain price is known as
    a. stock right.
    b. stock warrant.
    c. stock conversion.
    d. stock option.

14. Equity securities have the following right(s):
    a. right to share in the dividends
    b. right to vote
    c. right to a proportionate share of net assets upon liquidation of corporation
    d. all of the above

15. True or False. Insulating owners from a defectively formed corporation is known as the doctrine to corporation by estoppel.

16. True or False. The Revised Uniform Limited Partnership Act (RULPA) governs the formation of limited partnerships.

17. A joint stock company is
    a. formed after combining two or more corporations.
    b. members pooling capital into a common fund.
    c. considered the same as a corporation.
    d. a limited liability cooperative.

18. Combining debt securities and equity securities of a corporation is regarded as
    a. capital leverage.
    b. capital structure.
    c. paid-in capital.
    d. capital surplus.

19. True or False. Dividends are declared by stockholders.

20. Profits left in the corporation will be reported as _____ on the balance sheet of the corporation.
    a. paid-in capital
    b. capital surplus
    c. retained earnings
    d. undeclared dividends

21. A shareholder may aggregate his or her votes to elect directors by exercising his or her
    a. straight voting rights.
    b. cumulative voting rights.
    c. dissent voting rights.
    d. none of the above

22. True or False. A dissenting vote recorded in the minutes eliminates the dissenting director's potential personal liability for the action taken.

23. True or False. A de jure corporation is a corporation that has met all statutory requirements for its creation.

24. True or False. A usury rate is the excess over the lawful interest rate.

25. A(n) _____ is a corporate debt evidenced by a certificate of some type.
    a. stock share
    b. debenture
    c. escrow
    d. indemnification

CONTRACT LAW

Select the best answer for each of the following questions unless a specific group of questions instructs you to do otherwise.

1. True or False. A delegation generally requires the express consent of all parties.

2. True or False. If a contract is voidable by one party for lack of capacity due to intoxication and if that party later performs a portion of the contract while sober, the contract is no longer voidable.

3. True or False. The difference between a bilateral contract and a unilateral contract is the number of promises exchanged by the parties.

4. True or False. A contract generally is enforceable when there is a valid offer, there is a valid acceptance, and the agreement is supported by mutuality of assent.

5. Alan sends Baker an offer that reads, "We will sell you 4,000 white wicker chairs for $20 each. Reject or accept immediately." Baker responds, "We accept your offer but wish to have 4,000 natural wicker chairs instead." Baker has made a
    a. valid offer.
    b. valid acceptance.
    c. valid counteroffer.
    d. valid cross-offer.
    e. none of the above

6. In an attempt to sell his house to Baker, Alan states, "Buffalo Bill stayed here when he brought his Wild West Show to town." The truth is that Alan has no idea where Buffalo Bill might have stayed. Relying on this statement, Baker buys the house and then discovers the statement to have been false. Which of the following legal theories may be supported on these facts?
    a. fraud only
    b. either fraud or misrepresentation
    c. misrepresentation only
    d. none of the above

7. Bill and Mary visited Smokin' Joe's RV Sales to find a replacement vehicle for their 1960 Volkswagen van. Joe showed them a 1990 van and told them that it was the best used van on his lot. Bill and Mary bought the van and drove it off the lot; when they reached the corner intersection, the engine fell out. Which of the following statements is most correct?
    a. Bill and Mary can obtain contract damages for fraud against Joe.
    b. Bill and Mary can obtain rescission of the contract for Joe's misrepresentation.
    c. Bill and Mary can obtain restitution damages to prevent Joe's unjust enrichment.
    d. Bill and Mary can obtain nothing since Joe merely was puffing.

8. True or False. Under the U.C.C., if a merchant offeree adds terms to an offer before acceptance, the new terms will become part of the contract unless the offeror objects within a reasonable time.

9. True or False. A newspaper advertisement generally is treated as an offer to members of the public.

10. True or False. Alan promises to perform a service to Baker, in exchange for which Baker promises to file his (Alan) income tax return on April 15. Alan is not bound.

11. True or False. In certain circumstances, the U.C.C. may be applied to real estate sales transactions.

12. True or False. Alan agrees to buy all of the widgets that Baker can supply, provided that Alan is satisfied with the quality of the widgets. Alan's promise is not enforceable because it is illusory.

13. True or False. In general, the U.C.C. requires contracts for the sale of goods valued in excess of $250 to be in writing to be enforceable.

14. Sam agrees to refurbish a 1954 Packard automobile for Willie for $6,000. After deducting his costs, Sam anticipates a profit of $4,300. After Sam purchases the parts and completes almost all of the work, Willie appears in Sam's driveway and removes the car, saying that he has changed his mind. Willie then takes the car to Roscoe, who completes the car for $1,500. Which of the following is most accurate?
    a. Sam can recover nothing because he did not complete the work.
    b. Sam can recover $1,500 from Willie as contract damages.
    c. Sam can recover $4,300 from Willie as contract damages.
    d. Sam can recover $6,000 from Willie as contract damages.

15. True or False. When parties agree to substitute one performance for another in a contractual arrangement, an accord and satisfaction occurs.

16. True or False. When parties agree to substitute one party's performance for another's, an accord and satisfaction occurs.

17. True or False. Parol evidence rules apply to matters related to the meaning of contract terms, both before and after the creation of the contract.

18. True or False. Even in states where punitive damages are permitted, the damages typically are not awarded in commercial contract cases.

19. True or False. Under the U.C.C., when a buyer breaches, the seller may "cover" by purchasing substitute goods on the open market.

20. True or False. As a general rule, only a non-breaching party may recover contract damages.

21. True or False. Contracts for the sale of land must be in writing to be enforceable.

22. True or False. When one leaves clothing with a retail laundry, a master-servant contract is created.

23. True or False. Boarding a bus and putting money in the slot without saying anything is a type of quasi contract.

24. _____ is the common law term for today's quasi contract.
    a. Ad faciendum
    b. Assumpsit
    c. Fieri facias
    d. Ejusdem generis

25. One who wishes to transfer his or her rights under a valid contract should execute a(n)
    a. option.
    b. assignment.
    c. delegation.
    d. conveyance.

26. The document used to transfer legal ownership of personal property from one person to another when a title document is not required is a(n)
    a. invoice of purchase.
    b. power of attorney.
    c. bill of sale.
    d. conveyance transfer.

27. The term used to refer to a mere promise, sometimes called a bare promise, that (standing alone) cannot be enforced by the court is
    a. void.
    b. nudum pactum.
    c. nexus promisor.
    d. promisor initio.

Fill in the blank with the term or phrase that best fits the definition shown.

28. _____ deed that passes title only (no warranties)

CIVIL LITIGATION

Select the best answer for each of the following questions unless a specific group of questions instructs you to do otherwise.

1. True or False. A federal civil action is deemed commenced when the summons and complaint are served on the defendants.

2. True or False. In a federal civil case, venue refers to the district where an action can or should be tried.

3. True or False. The U.S. District Court is a federal court of general jurisdiction.

4. True of False. Parties must be from different states before a federal district court may exercise federal question jurisdiction.

5. True or False. A temporary restraining order may be granted ex parte.

6. True or False. A preliminary injunction may be granted ex parte.

7. True or False. All relevant evidence is admissible unless otherwise provided by the Constitution, by statute, by the Federal Rules of Evidence, or by some other primary authority.

8. True or False. Hearsay evidence is not admissible unless a specific exception exists under the Federal Rules of Evidence.

9. True or False. Evidence that a defendant offered to compromise a claim is not admissible to prove liability in a lawsuit concerning the same claim.

10. True or False. Ben was injured when he tripped on a cracked sidewalk in front of the Easy Suds Laundromat. In a civil suit by Ben against the laundromat, evidence that the laundromat repaired the sidewalk soon after Ben's injury probably is admissible on the issue of liability.

11. Which of the following tasks is a paralegal not likely to perform?
    a. draft proposed questions for a deposition
    b. attend a deposition
    c. ask questions at a deposition
    d. digest and summarize a deposition

12. Proper venue in a federal civil action may not be based on which of the following?
    a. where the plaintiffs reside
    b. where all of the defendants reside
    c. where a substantial part of the claim arose or where the subject property is located
    d. where all defendants can be served at the time of filing

13. A party to a federal civil action may obtain records from non-party witnesses by using which of the following discovery devices?
    a. Rule 34 request to produce documents
    b. Rule 45 subpoena duces tecum
    c. Rule 30 deposition
    d. none of the above

14. If a defendant files a motion for a more definite statement under Rule 12 and if the motion is granted, how long does the defendant have to serve his or her responsive pleading following the plaintiff's filing of a more definite statement?
    a. ten days
    b. fifteen days
    c. twenty days
    d. thirty days

15. Which of the following discovery devices may not be used in connection with a non-party?
    a. interrogatories
    b. subpoena duces tecum
    c. deposition
    d. none of the above
    e. all of the above

16. Civil actions in the federal courts use which of the following forms of pleading?
    a. code pleading
    b. fact pleading
    c. notice pleading
    d. federal rules pleading

17. A summons in a federal civil action may be issued by
    a. the court clerk.
    b. the U.S. Marshal's office.
    c. the attorney for the plaintiff.
    d. anyone over the age of eighteen who is not a party.
    e. all of the above

18. After each party has concluded his or her case in a federal civil trial, either party may request that judgment be entered for him or her without submitting the case to the jury by
    a. motion for directed verdict.
    b. motion for judgment as a matter of law.
    c. summary judgment.
    d. none of the above

19. At the conclusion of a federal civil trial, a party may, in certain situations, ask the court to "overrule" the jury verdict by requesting a
    a. new trial.
    b. judgment notwithstanding the verdict.
    c. directed verdict.
    d. judgment as a matter of law.

20. A motion for new trial in federal court must be filed within
    a. ten days after entry of judgment.
    b. twenty days after entry of judgment.
    c. thirty days after entry of judgment.
    d. forty five days after entry of judgment.

21. True or False. Motion for new trial is a prerequisite for appeal in federal court.

22. True or False. Enforcement of a judgment may be stayed pending appeal by entry of an order of stay coupled with the filing of a supersedeas bond.

23. True or False. A statute of frauds provides that unless a cause of action is filed within a stated period of time, it is barred forever. This is to prevent fraud by a would-be plaintiff.

24. A sworn statement of the truth of facts stated in a particular document, instrument, or pleading is a(n)
    a. affidavit.
    b. acknowledgment.
    c. verification.
    d. certification.

25. If a party seeks the appearance of another to give testimony and to produce certain documents, the party should have the would-be testifier served with a
    a. subpoena.
    b. subpoena duces tecum.
    c. summons.
    d. notice to take depositions.

26. A separate issue or matter arising from or related to a tort is
    a. de son tort.
    b. et sequenti.
    c. ex delicto.
    d. ex post facto.

27. The common law remedy for return of personal property that is held unlawfully by another is
    a. restitution.
    b. bailment.
    c. replevin.
    d. assumpsit.

Fill in each blank with the term or phrase that best fits the definition shown.

28. _____ written defamation

29. _____ and others

30. _____ reduction or termination

31. _____ failure to use the care of a reasonable person

CERTIFIED PARALEGAL PROGRAM MOCK EXAMINATION ANSWER KEY

COMMUNICATIONS

1.	was	30.	a
2.	ensure	31.	e
3.	elude	32.	a
4.	bad	33.	b
5.	Most	34.	d
6.	c	35.	a
7.	b	36.	b
8.	b	37.	a
9.	a	38.	c
10.	d	39.	c
11.	c	40.	b
12.	a	41.	c
13.	d	42.	a
14.	d	43.	c
15.	c	44.	b
16.	b	45.	a
17.	a	46.	a
18.	b	47.	b
19.	a	48.	b
20.	a	49.	b
21.	a	50.	a
22.	b	51.	nuncupative
23.	a	52.	sui generic
24.	a	53.	True
25.	b	54.	True
26.	a	55.	False
27.	b	56.	False
28.	a	57.	False
29.	a	58.	False

JUDGMENT AND ANALYTICAL ABILITY

1.	c	10.	a
2.	d	11.	b
3.	a	12.	b
4.	b	13.	a
5.	d	14.	a
6.	a	15.	False
7.	b	16.	True
8.	c	17.	True
9.	d	18.	a

19. d	30. c
20. d	31. b
21. b	32. c
22. d	33. b
23. True	34. c
24. False	35. c
25. False	36. c
26. True	37. a
27. c	38. b
28. a	39. d
29. c	40. a

ETHICS

1. c	25. False
2. True	26. d
3. d	27. False
4. c	28. True
5. d	29. False
6. d	30. b
7. d	31. True
8. True	32. False
9. True	33. False
10. False	34. False
11. b	35. e
12. d	36. d
13. c	37. False
14. True	38. False
15. False	39. c
16. True	40. False
17. d	41. False
18. b	42. True
19. c	43. True
20. False	44. False
21. True	45. False
22. e	46. True
23. e	47. True
24. c	48. True

LEGAL RESEARCH

1. False	10. True
2. True	11. b
3. True	12. d
4. True	13. a
5. True	14. b
6. False	15. d
7. True	16. c
8. True	17. a
9. False	18. d

19. c
20. a
21. True
22. False
23. False
24. True
25. True
26. False
27. False
28. True
29. False
30. False
31. a
32. b
33. b
34. d
35. a
36. c
37. b
38. b
39. b
40. c
41. a
42. c
43. a
44. True
45. True
46. False
47. True
48. d
49. a
50. c
51. inter alia
52. non obstante
53. non sequitur
54. nota bene (N.B)

SUBSTANTIVE LAW

General Law—American Legal System

1. False
2. False
3. False
4. True
5. True
6. True
7. False
8. False
9. False
10. True
11. b
12. f
13. d
14. b
15. a
16. c
17. b
18. a
19. a
20. d
21. False
22. False
23. True
24. True
25. True
26. False
27. False
28. True
29. False
30. False
31. b
32. d
33. d
34. c
35. d
36. False
37. False
38. True
39. a
40. b
41. summons
42. perjury
43. motion

Business Organizations

1. False
2. b
3. d
4. b
5. True
6. b
7. c
8. b
9. d
10. True
11. False
12. False
13. d
14. d
15. True
16. True
17. b
18. b
19. False
20. c
21. b
22. True
23. True
24. True
25. b

Contract Law

1. True
2. True
3. True
4. False
5. c
6. b
7. d
8. True
9. False
10. True
11. False
12. False
13. False
14. d
15. True
16. False
17. False
18. True
19. False
20. True
21. True
22. False
23. False
24. b
25. b
26. c
27. b
28. quitclaim

Civil Litigation

1. False
2. True
3. False
4. False
5. True
6. False
7. True
8. True
9. True
10. False
11. c
12. a
13. b
14. a
15. a
16. c
17. a
18. b
19. d
20. a
21. False
22. True
23. False
24. c
25. b
26. c
27. c
28. libel
29. et al.
30. abatement
31. negligence